MW01514838

Friday Night Lights for Fathers and Sons

Friday Night Lights for Fathers and Sons

**SCHEDULE A 10-GAME WINNING SEASON TO HELP DEVELOP
YOUR SON INTO THE MAN GOD INTENDED HIM TO BE**

Mark LaMaster

AUTHOR ACADEMY elite

5-4-2018

Copyright © 2015 Mark LaMaster
All rights reserved.

Printed in the United States of America

Published by Author Academy Elite
P.O. Box 43, Powell, OH 43035
www.AuthorAcademyElite.com

All rights reserved. No part of this publication may be reproduced, stored in a
retrieval system, or transmitted in any form or by any means—for example, electronic,
photocopy, recording—without the prior written permission of the publisher. The only
exception is brief quotations in printed reviews.

ISBN: 1943526095
ISBN 13: 9781943526093
Library of Congress Control Number: 2015917519
Author Academy Elite, Powell, OH

Unless otherwise indicated, Scripture quotations are from the Holy Bible, New
International Version®, NIV®, Copyright© 1973, 1978, 1984, 2011 by Biblica, Inc.™ Used by
permission of Zondervan. All rights reserve worldwide, www.zondervan.com

Imagine being a coach coming to a game when your team has had no practice, no preparation, not even a playbook...it would hardly be worth showing up. Yet that's how many men approach fatherhood with their sons. LaMaster's *Friday Night Lights for Fathers and Sons* provides a playbook through some of the toughest fatherhood topics we must teach our sons – topics ranging from integrity to Internet and porn addiction. Each topic is creatively designed to engage conversation between father and son while making memories that last a lifetime. As fathers, we must be the coach to develop our sons into the man that God designed them to be. Pick up your copy of *Friday Night Lights for Fathers and Sons* and schedule your 10 game season today!

Ron DeHaas
President and Founder, Covenant Eyes
www.covenanteyes.com

As I was reading *Friday Night Lights for Fathers and Sons*, I often found myself thinking about the time my dad invested in me and the great times we have had. This book will help me be intentional about the time I spend with our son. I could feel the Holy Spirit speaking with every page I read! God is and will continue to use *Friday Night Lights for Fathers and Sons* to transform boys into courageous men of God and men into dads that are warriors.

Robb Ammermann
Pastor of Student Ministries
Christ Community Church

As a pediatrician, I know firsthand that many dads want to spend more intentional time with their sons—but aren't sure what to do. LaMaster's *Friday Night Lights for Fathers and Sons* provides a practical, biblically based game plan for dads to help guide their sons through the challenging tween years. Each Game Day is practical, purposeful, and will have a powerful impact on both fathers and sons.

Jason (Jay) Homme, M.D.
Pediatrics and Adolescent Medicine,
Rochester, MN

Mark LaMaster's book "Friday Night Lights for Fathers and Sons" offers interesting and inventive ways for fathers to teach their sons biblical truths about using money, being content, staying away from pornography, working and many other topics. This book gives men the tools they need to help their sons develop into godly men.

Amber Albee Swenson
Author of Bible Moms:
Life Lessons from Mothers in the Bible

For Lincoln.
You make my life better
because you are in it.
God has an amazing plan for you.
I love you and am so proud of the
young man you are becoming.

Contents

* Please read Special Note at beginning of this chapter.

Foreword

The world needs strong men and a bunch more of them. These men must feel fully, lead boldly, and serve wholeheartedly. They must love God and people.

While it's easy to pontificate about such a need, Mark LaMaster did something about this need. First—although imperfect like the rest of us—he, with the help of his Savior Jesus Christ, decided to become that type of man himself.

Secondly, he decided to help other men demystify the process by distilling his model into a simple handbook for fathers and sons. We now finally have a Game Plan for dads to help develop their sons into the men God intended them to be.

Many fathers and sons crave a stronger connection with each other and their God. Unfortunately, most of the time, we're just not sure how to do this. *Friday Night Lights for Fathers and Sons* provides the answer. Discover how to schedule a 10-Game Day season with your son. Each Game Day is designed to engage dads and their sons in conversation on topics ranging from faith and friends to prayer and purity.

Introduction

Intention without action is only a dream.
— MARK SANBORN

Don't get me wrong—I consider myself a "good" dad. But I want to be a GREAT dad! Ever since I took Robert Lewis' Authentic Manhood: Winning at Home and at Work course, I was awakened to the fact that I needed to be *intentional* about how I fathered my two young children. Lewis taught me to look to the Bible for parenting advice.[1] Whether or not I was living in a cave for the past thirty something years or was just naïve, I am not sure. But ever since Robert Lewis discussed Proverbs 22:6, I have been a dad on a mission to be the best dad that I can be.

Train up a child in the way he should go,
and he will not depart from it.
— PROVERBS 22:6

I started reading book after book about how to become a better dad. In fact, I spent more time reading about how to become a great Christian dad than actually doing the things necessary to become a great dad. Can you identify? It's not much different than reading diet books and never starting the diet or reading a financial planning book and never saving any money.

As I said, there are many excellent Christian parenting books for all of us dads to read. In fact, I have created the "Fatherhood Personnel File" reading list for you at the back of the book. We are blessed to have so many amazing authors to provide many invaluable parenting resources that, quite simply, were not available even a generation ago.

I talked to my dad about what he used for parenting resources. He pointed to Dr. Spock's *Baby and Child Care*, first published in 1946, and Dr. Dodson's *How to Parent*, from 1971.[2,3] When I became a father over 12 years ago, my dad gave me his copy of *How to Father*, also by Dr. Dodson.[4] This was a great read, but I wanted something a bit more current.

Let's fast forward to present day. Simply typing in the words "parenting" in the Amazon.com book section reveals 105,000 results with over 3,000 results listed as best sellers and 55 results as best sellers in 2015 alone.[5] What about "parenting" and "Christian"? This search brings up 7,539 results. So from a handful of books in our parents' generation to literally thousands of books today, many dads might now be wondering why Mark LaMaster thinks his book will have anything to offer. Great question! Let me explain.

I absolutely enjoy spending time with my kids. In fact, spending time with my family reenergizes me after a busy day at work, with friends, or while working on various projects at home. I guess I would classify myself as a "homebody." Homebody, as defined by the Merriam-Webster Dictionary, is "one whose life centers on home." This would certainly describe me. Unfortunately, I was curious and decided to look at other definitions as well. Here's how the Google Dictionary defines homebody: "a person who likes to stay at home...one who is perceived as unadventurous." Wow! That one kind of made me think. I truly am not an adventurous guy. I don't hunt, fish, camp, or bungee jump—you get the idea. Upon reflection of my day-to-day life, I truly am a homebody, an unadventurous dad whose life centers on my home.

So after taking Lewis' Authentic Manhood: Winning at Home and at Work course, reading several parenting books and a handful of father and son books, I became intentional about becoming a better father to my son.[1] I wanted to lead him toward his God-given "bent," or his talents and blessings from God. The problem was I had no idea what to do with my son that would allow me to focus on what it takes to become a man of God. What questions do I ask him? What Bible verses will guide me to the teachable moments that arise? What topics do I want to highlight during my dedicated time with my son?

I know that my son wants me to spend time with him, no matter what we do. I love going to his sporting events, watching Nebraska football (Go Big Red!), going to a movie, going out for wings, reading with him, praying with him before he goes to bed, and all of the things a dad does on a daily basis. However, I am the type of guy who needs some type of plan. I wanted to have a game plan for our dedicated time together that involved the Bible, characteristics of becoming a man of God, and having fun!

The only problem is I had no idea where to start. So I looked for books on parenting that could help me with my dilemma, but I could not find what I was looking for. Don't get me wrong. I just shared with you that there are over 105,000 books on parenting. But I decided to take my Amazon.com search a little further. Here is what I found:

Of the over 105,000 parenting books listed in Amazon, 2,695 were listed for "parenting books and fathers." Only 601 books were listed for "parenting books and fathers and sons." I then decided to type in "father and son dates." This search resulted in 196 books. Lastly, I searched "parenting books and Christian and fathers and sons." To my surprise, this yielded only 96 books.[5]

So let's see what books are out there for mothers and daughters. By replacing father and son with mother and daughter, here are the results: "parenting books and mothers" – 6,792; "parenting books for mothers and daughters" –

860; "mother and daughter dates" – 296; "parenting books and Christian and mothers and daughters" – 121.[5]

So according to my not-so-scientific research on Amazon.com, only 96 books exist that are Christian based and focus on fathers and sons. Whether this is absolutely accurate or not, it helped me prove to myself that my pursuit for the kind of resource I wanted was not available. Over the next couple of years, despite being intentional about dedicating focused time with my son, I did not take action on my intentions.

One day while my wife and I were talking about my dilemma, she said, "Why don't you write your own book?" The thought went in and out of my mind in about one minute. I consciously told myself that I was not an author.

Then it happened! We have all heard testimonies how God has spoken into people's lives, but it had truly never happened to me. I have been a believer in Jesus Christ since I can remember and know that He has guided me to where I am today. He has blessed me immeasurably and has provided me with an amazing family, a great job, and my health. However, I don't remember anything ever happening like it did in the middle of a cold winter night in early 2014.

To set the stage, Jen had traveled out of town to help her friend celebrate her baby shower. Jen and I rarely spend a night apart, but this was a dear college friend who had tried for several years to become pregnant and finally did. It was not only a baby shower but also a college reunion, a girls' night out, and a celebration of God's blessings. The kids and I had spent Friday evening making dinner and watching a movie. Because Jen was gone, the kids wanted to fall asleep in our room. I decided to stay up for a while and read. The next thing I knew, I heard a voice saying, "Write the book." I was only half awake and tried to fall back asleep. Again, I heard a deep voice saying, "Write the book." I sat up in bed just to make sure no one was actually in my room, shook out the cobwebs, and confirmed that I truly wasn't dreaming and that there was no one else in my house.

I did not hear the voice again, but I had a strange sensation wash over me, a sensation that is difficult to describe with words. The sensation led me to my computer at 1:45 in the morning to begin writing this book. That night the concept for the title of this book was created, not by me but through the power of the Holy Spirit. I don't know how to explain it and am not sure if I am supposed to. What I can say is that less than a week before my wife and I put together a prayer journal inspired by Stormie Omartian and Lisa Whelchel.

I was called to "write the book" to help dads like you and me have a resource that will provide structure to dedicated father and son time based on the biblical definition of men.

Whether or not the book sells or is successful in this world, I have decided to listen to the words that God spoke to me in the middle of a frigid, Minnesota night. The words of this book have been typed by Mark LaMaster but were inspired by the Word of God.

So, dads, get off the bench, dust off your cleats, and schedule a 10-game winning season with your son today to strengthen your father–son relationship, to become closer to God, and to help lead your son to become the man God designed him to be!

Pre-Season

We are born male. We must learn to be men.

— KENT NERBURN

CHAPTER 1

Pre-Season Self-Scouting Report

Are you a benchwarmer dad, or are you in the starting lineup?

A few years ago, I decided to take my son to a local high school base-ball game. It was a particularly blustery Minnesota spring after-noon. We thought we were pretty cool wearing shorts despite the fact that we were also wearing a sweatshirt and jacket to protect us from near gale-force winds. As we surveyed the bleachers, there were only a couple of spots left, even though we arrived during pre-game warm-ups. My son, Lincoln, and I strutted up the bleachers and maneuvered into two open spots between a couple of other guys.

The home team took the field, and soon the catcher yelled, "Comin' down," and threw a perfect throw to second base. With that, the home plate umpire directed the leadoff batter to the plate to start the game. Before I knew it, the two guys that Lincoln and I had squeezed between, as well as about 10 other guys, pulled out their radar guns and aimed them at home plate. I knew that this particular pitcher was being scouted, but what I didn't know was that Lincoln and I would be sitting amongst 10–15 Major League Baseball scouts. Soon, Lincoln and I were able to catch a peek at the numbers popping up on their radar guns: 96, 97, and an occasional 98 mph. Lincoln and I shared a mem-ory that windy Wednesday afternoon, huddled between Major League scouts.

The pitcher was drafted to the big leagues and signed a six-figure contract. He is still working his way to "The Show" but continues to improve. Every once in a while, I still see his name appear in our local newspaper.

This memory with Lincoln made me think of how I would be rated as a dad by a Major League scout. As I shared with you before, I took a good, long look at what kind of father I was several years back. I began reading as much as I could on how to become a better dad. The only problem was that I had great intentions and strategies but lacked action.

I would like you to take the Self-Scouting Survey I have developed to help you better understand what kind of dad you are right now. When answering the questions, be honest with yourself. Don't answer the questions on how you want to be or should be as a dad. The purpose of this survey is to help you identify where you are now as a dad.

Pre-Season Self-Scouting Survey

Please circle the answer that best describes you as the dad you are today.

1. During the typical weekday, I spend an average of _____ with my son.
    a. between 30 and 60 minutes
    b. greater than 2 hours
    c. less than 30 minutes
    d. between 1 and 2 hours

2. During a typical weekend, I spend an average of _____ with my son.
    a. between 1 and 2 hours
    b. greater than 4 hours
    c. less than 1 hour
    d. between 2 and 4 hours

3. I tuck my son into bed an average of _____ nights per week.
    a. 3–5
    b. 6–7
    c. 0–1
    d. 1–3

4. The last time I said, "I love you," to my son was _____.
    a. yesterday
    b. today
    c. I can't remember
    d. last month

5. The most recent time I prayed with my son was _____.
    a. last week
    b. last night
    c. I can't remember
    d. last month

6. When was the last time you planned an event or activity with just you and your son?
    a. last month
    b. last week
    c. never
    d. last year

7. When my son needs help with homework, I _____.
    a. usually help him
    b. stop what I am doing and help him
    c. have his mom, brother, or sister help him
    d. try to help him but then get distracted or frustrated

8. I carve out time in my day to talk to my son about his concerns related to friend issues, expected body changes, and other difficult topics:

    a.   I schedule time a couple of times a year.

    b.   I both schedule time and take time to talk to him as situations arise.

    c.   I let his mother handle those things.

    d.   I have tried this several times, but I am just not good at this kind of stuff.

9.   I take my family to church _____.

    a.   about 2 times per month

    b.   every Sunday, with rare exceptions

    c.   on Easter and Christmas Eve

    d.   several times per year between my son's sports seasons

10. I read the Bible _____.

    a.   a few days a week

    b.   every day

    c.   rarely, if ever

    d.   once a month, maybe

You did it! You completed the Self-Scouting Survey. Next, count up all of the d's you circled, and enter that number next to the letter below. Then do the same for the c's, b's, and a's.

d _____ c _____ b_____ a_____

All right, the moment of truth. Determine which letter you have the most of, and circle the letter below to determine the type of dad you are right now. After reading this book and going through the 10-Game Season with your son, I truly believe you will become a Playoff Dad!

B. Playoff Dad

    Strong work! I would love to hear from you on how you became a Playoff Dad! Don't change a thing.

A. Starting Lineup Dad

Congratulations! You have made the starting lineup, Dad! With continued focus, intention, and action, you will make the playoffs soon.

D. 6th Man Dad

You are on the right track! You have earned your spot to become the first man off the bench! I am confident that you will find several resources in the 10-Game Season to work your way towards the playoffs.

C. Benchwarmer Dad

No worries, Dad! The fact that you are reading this book shows me that you want to become a better dad. This book is going to help you greatly!

CHAPTER 2

Fatherhood Stats and Clock Management Considerations for Dads

Do you know what the ticker line stats are on fatherhood in America today?

Let's face it, dads, many of us are numbers guys. We love stats. We love watching ESPN and keeping track of this year's top running backs, points leaders, home run hitters, batting averages, and so on. Perhaps you just like numbers or are involved with a friendly, competitive game of fantasy football.

Unfortunately, the following fatherlessness statistics in the United States are anything but fantasy. Check out the the brow-raising statistics below:

- 24.7 million children (33%) live in homes without their biological father.[1]
- 57.6% of black children, 31.2% of Hispanic children, and 20.7% of white children are living without their biological father.[2]
- 71% of all high school dropouts come from fatherless homes.[3]
- 71% of all pregnant teenagers come from fatherless homes.[3]
- 90% of all homeless and runaway children come from fatherless homes.[3]

- 63% of youth suicides come from fatherless homes.[3]
- 85% of all children with behavior disorders come from fatherless homes.[3]
- 85% of all youth in prison come from fatherless homes.[3]

The National Center for Fathering's (NCF) website has a link to the trailer for the documentary, *Irreplaceable*. During the trailer, Carey Casey, NCF's founder and CEO, describes the impact of fathers in the lives of their children. In one clip, Casey shares how many athletes he knows who simply want to see their fathers in the stands—nothing more, nothing less.[3]

These stats are painful and sobering to read. Some of us have come from traditional two-parent families and take for granted how vital the father role has been in our lives. Sadly, some of us come from broken homes and completely understand how the above stats have reached record highs. Others of us come from two-parent families, but our fathers were absent in one way or another. Regardless of whether you grew up with a father or not, live with your son now, or are not living with your son, you have the choice to become a part of his life. You must be intentional and focused with the time you have left before your son goes out on his own.

When I look forward to April, I think of my birthday, my wife's birthday, Easter, the Masters, and finally, the NFL Draft. Each April, after two months without football, the NFL holds its annual draft. ESPN analysts discuss every detail, projection, and mock draft possible. Soon, all of the speculation subsides as the NFL commissioner struts across the stage and steps up to the microphone. As he introduces the team with the first pick of the first round, the commissioner officially starts the draft with these words: "You are now on the clock." Dads, you are all officially "on the clock" for your sons. The clock has been ticking since the day your son was born.

What amazes me is how truly fast time really does go! As dads, we think we have all of the time in the world to teach our sons all of the things we want to teach them. In less than 10 years, my son will be graduating from high school and, I hope, will be heading off to college, trade school, or the military. I know that I will always be his dad, but I only have 10 years left to tuck him into bed each night and to teach him all the things I want to teach him before he enters the next stage in his life.

Dads, we are "on the clock" with our sons. Life does not have timeouts and replays. We don't get to go to the replay booth to change the poor choices we have made as fathers. We don't have coaches and trainers pushing us to be the best dads that we can possibly be. We don't have full-ride scholarships or multi-million-dollar contracts to compensate us for being the best dad. Wow, that's depressing, isn't it? As Lee Corso from ESPN's *College GameDay* says, "Not so fast, my friends." But, dads, we actually have someone on our coaching staff who far surpasses all of the legendary coaches combined. Anyone have a guess?

God.

God provides us with all of the tools we need to be the dads He wants us to be. In his book, *King Me*, Steve Farrar shares God's job description for fathers as illustrated by Deuteronomy 6:5–7 (NIV):

> *You shall love the Lord your God with all your heart and soul and with all your might. These words, which I am commanding you today, shall be on your heart. You shall teach them diligently to your sons and shall talk of them when you sit in your house and when you walk by the way and when you lie down and when you rise up.*

To summarize, God's job description for us dads is to:

1) Love God deeply.
2) Teach our son diligently.[4]

You are not alone in your journey as a father, but you are "on the clock." God is with you every step of the way, but you have to get off the bench, off the sidelines, and into the game of fatherhood. Your son needs you now. Tick tock, tick tock, tick tock...

Dads, I would encourage you to take a few moments now to calculate the number of nights you have left to tuck your son into bed while knowing that he is under the same roof. No matter your son's age, the number of years until your son graduates from high school may seem like a long way off. In reality, each day that passes is an opportunity to help mold him into the man you and God want him to become. My son is ten years old. I know that he graduates from high school in 9 years. That's only 3,285 days. With this perspective in mind, my hope is that the time you spend with your son during *Friday Night Lights for Fathers and Sons* will inspire you to spend hundreds of more hours with him.

Have you ever heard of the 4–14 Window? No, it's not the size of the window a professional quarterback has to throw the football between the linebackers and defensive backs. And no, it's not a play call that one of the Manning brothers uses at the line of scrimmage.

According to an article by Dan Brewster in 2005, a study by the International Bible Society indicated that 83% of all Christians in the United States make their commitment to Jesus Christ between the ages of 4 and 14 years. The article goes on to state that youth or teens aged 14 to 18 years only have a 4% probability of accepting Jesus. If your son is between 4 and 14 and has not heard of Jesus Christ and has not accepted Him as his Savior, now is the time for you to act![5]

There is one more set of statistics that I feel strongly about sharing with you. In a 1994 Swiss-based study, respondents were asked to determine whether or not they believed a person's religion carried through to the next generation—and if so, why or why not?

The results might surprise you!

- If the father is non-practicing and the mother is a regular church attender, only 2 percent of children will become church worshippers.
- If the father is a regular church attender and the mother is not, 38% of children will become regular church attenders.
- If a father does not go to church, no matter how faithful his wife's devotions, only one child in 50 will become a regular worshipper.[6]

The critical factor that is revealed in this study is that it is the religious practice of the father of the family that, above all, determines the future attendance at or absence from church of the children.

Now that you know what kind of dad you are right now, are up to date on the most recent fatherlessness stats, and are now officially on the clock, are you ready to begin your pre-season preparations for *Friday Night Lights* with your son?

CHAPTER 3

A Father's Pre-Season Preparation Plan

Your guide to using Friday Night Lights for Fathers and Sons

We are almost ready to begin the Regular Season of *Friday Night Lights for Fathers and Sons*, but before we get started, I want to give a brief overview of this season's strategy. In order for you to get the most out of this season, I thought a few pointers would help make it go a bit smoother.

Each Game Day is divided into the following 11 sections:

- Game Plan
- God's Key Play
- Scouting Report for Dads
- Pre-Game Planning
- Pre-Game Day Prayer
- Playbook
- Audible Options
- Post-Game Day Analysis
- Post-Game Day Press Conference

- Link's X's and O's
- Post-Game Day Prayer

Let's break each section down now!

Game Plan

The Game Plan serves as a quick overview for each Game Day—the Game Day Theme, God's Key Play, and the Game Day Activity.

God's Key Play

Each Game Day has a Bible verse that I have named God's Key Play. This Bible verse was specifically chosen to help illustrate each Game Day's primary objective. God's Key Play will be referred to multiple times during each Game Day. Dads, I challenge you to memorize each of God's Key Plays!

Scouting Report for Dads

All great teams scout their opponent to learn their strategies, strong players, and sneak plays. The Scouting Report for Dads provides insight into each Game Day theme. This is meant to be read by dads for the purpose of providing key information in discussions with your son during each Game Day activity.

Pre-Game Planning

Without proper planning, your Game Day may be an epic failure. The purpose of the Pre-Game Planning is to help you prepare the necessary materials and review the information to help ensure each Game Day is a success.

Pre-Game Day Prayer

I have written the Pre-Game Prayers for you to begin each Game Day with. Many of us do not feel comfortable praying out loud or are not comfortable praying at all. For those of you that would rather pray on your own, know that my prayer is a template only. You will notice that I have left space for your son's name to make it as personal as possible.

Playbook

The Playbook is a step-by-step plan to assist you in leading you and your son to a winning game! I have done my best to lead you in a chronological and logical process to make the most impact for both you and your son. Again, this is to be used only as a guide. If you so choose to add, edit, or delete a step or two, you will be forgiven! At the end of the day, this book is about you and your son spending time together.

Audible Options

To help emphasize my previous point, I have created Audible Options for most of the Game Day activities if you are limited by cost, interest, or ability. Feel free to share any of your personally created Audible Options on the Friday Night Lights for Fathers and Sons Facebook page.

Post-Game Day Analysis

Let's admit it. None of us are perfect. The best way to learn is from reviewing our mistakes. I created questions in the Post-Game Day Analysis for you and your son to review the more personal information together in an area where your conversation can be confidential. I believe that most of your relationship growth with your son and with God will happen during this time. I would encourage you to honestly answer each of the Post-Game Day Analysis questions.

Post-Game Day Press Conference

I have to admit that this is one of my favorite parts of the book! How cool would it be to sit at the press conference table with the microphone in front of you, cameras surrounding you, and your team's logo filling the background of the camera shot and dozens of reporters eager to ask YOU questions about your performance during today's game.

The Post-Game Day Press Conference has about four questions for both you and your son to answer on camera. You will need your smartphone with video camera or your digital video camera for each Post-Game Day Press Conference (aka "Presser"). You and your son will take turns answering the questions provided and will record each other's answers on video. This video will be used later for the Award Ceremony after the season is completed.

I encourage you to be creative with the Pressers! You can share your creative ideas on the Friday Night Lights for Fathers and Sons Facebook page.

Link's X's and O's

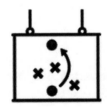

My son Lincoln (Link) was eager to help me write this book. Link's X's and O's section is a compilation of Lincoln's favorite things about each Game Day. Lincoln is 10 years old and wanted to share his excitement and the lessons he learned with your son from a kid's perspective. Lincoln would love to hear your son's X's and O's from your Game Day experiences as well. You can post them on the Friday Night Lights for Fathers and Sons Facebook page if you would like to share.

Post-Game Day Prayer

We want to give glory and thanks to God both before and after each Game Day experience. I have written a Post-Game Day Prayer for each Game Day and cannot think of a better way to close out a wonderful father and son experience.

Surveys

You will also see a few surveys and questionnaires throughout this book. Please take a few minutes to complete these important items. They will only take a couple of minutes but will provide valuable information for both you and your son.

Well, that about does it. Cue the opening music, get ready to run out onto the field, call heads or tails, and get ready for kickoff. Your 10-game season with your son is about to begin.

Regular Season

> Don't ever let someone tell you that you can't do
> something. Not even me. You got a dream, you
> gotta protect it. When people can't do something
> themselves, they're gonna tell you that you can't
> do it. You want something, go get it. Period.
> — CHRISTOPHER GARNDNER (THE PURSUIT OF HAPPYNESS)

GAME DAY 1

"Aim Small, Miss Small"

What does it mean to be a man with character and integrity?

Game Plan

Game Day Theme: Character and Integrity

God's Key Play: Matthew 7:13–14

Game Day Activity: Laser Tag

God's Key Play

*Enter through the narrow gate. For wide is the gate
and broad is the road that leads to destruction, and
many enter through it. But small is the gate and narrow
the road that leads to life, and only a few find it.*
— MATTHEW 7:13–14

Scouting Report for Dads

One of my all-time favorite movies is *The Patriot*, starring Mel Gibson. For those of you that have not seen the movie, this historical fiction movie takes place in 1776 at the height of the Revolutionary War. Gibson plays Benjamin Martin, a widowed father of seven young children, three of whom are old enough to be interested in fighting for the revolution. The viewer is aware that Martin is a war hero from the French and Indian War, but now that he is a family man, he wants to forget about the past and focus on raising his family.

Unfortunately, the war literally ends up in Martin's front yard. As the movie progresses, events force Martin to become involved with the war. One of his first acts is to order two of his young sons to kill British officers that have taken their oldest brother prisoner.

With only a few minutes to prepare his young sons, Martin gives them the following instructions:

> **Martin:** It's a good spot. Boys, listen to me. I'll fire first. I want you two to start with the officers and work your way down. Can you tell the difference?

> **Nathan & Samuel:** Yes, father. Yes, father.

> **Martin:** Good. Samuel, after your first shot, I want you to reload for your brother Nathan. Now, if anything should happen to me, I want you two to drop your weapons, and I want you to run as quickly as you can, you hide in the brush, make your way home, get your brother and sisters, and take them to Aunt Charlotte's. Understood? What did I tell you fellas about shooting?

> **Nathan & Samuel:** Aim small, miss small.

Martin: Aim small, miss small. Boys. Samuel. Steady. Lord, make me fast and accurate.[1]

What's cool to me is that it is obvious that Martin has spent time training up his boys on how to shoot, how to identify enemy officers, and where to meet in the event of an emergency, and he asks the Lord for help. If you have not seen this movie, I highly recommend it. It is chock full of how to be a God-fearing father!

For this Game Day, I want to focus on the implications that "aim small, miss small" has in leading you and your son to a Christian life with character and integrity. What does "aim small, miss small" mean? "Aim small, miss small" means that you should pick the tightest possible target, and even if you miss that target, you're still going to be very close to your goal. Just as Benjamin Martin taught his boys about shooting, we can teach our boys about their actions and decisions in life. We will never make the right decisions all the time, but if we follow God's plan, we can still hit our target.

Pre-Game Planning

Congratulations on taking the first step to carving out time in your busy schedule to spend intentional time with your son! The first game of the season is always important in setting the tone for the rest of the season, but don't worry if everything doesn't go as planned; you might be surprised at what you learn about yourself or about your son that was not part of the game plan!

All right, let's start planning for the first game of the season. The first Game Day activity is laser tag. If you do not have laser tag in your town or city, don't worry; I will have a list of alternate activities (Audible Options) below for you to choose from that will work just as well.

Here is a list of things for dads to do before Game Day #1:

1. Read Matthew 7:13–14.

   I also challenge you to memorize these verses. Not only will your son be impressed but you will be amazed at how powerful having these verses in your back pocket will be in future situations for yourself or for your son. If you complete this 10-game winning season and memorize each Game Day verse, you will already have memorized 10 verses of powerful Scripture.

2. Reflect on one or two decisions you have made in your life that were difficult and challenging but ended up being the right decision. Why? Because your son will most likely ask you some form of this question. If he doesn't, you will be able to share an example from your life to help start a deeper conversation with him.

   Here are some possible examples:

   a) When you said no to friends that asked you to drink alcohol, smoke a cigarette, or try drugs.
   b) When you said no to a girlfriend that wanted to go too far sexually.
   c) When you stood up for a classmate that your friends were bullying.
   d) When you turned down a promotion at work that required increased travel so you could have more time with your family.

These are just a few ideas to get your mind thinking and to help you brainstorm specific ideas that you have personally experienced.

3. Pray for the Holy Spirit to guide your thoughts, words, and actions as you embark on this season with your son.

4. Check out the nearest laser tag arena. To complete today's Game Day activity, you only need to play one game. Be prepared to play a couple more games because you or your son will want to play again!

While reading through Matthew 7:13–14, you have learned that the path to heaven is small and narrow. Well, what does this have to do with leading your son to a Christian life full of character and integrity? And what in the world does this have to do with laser tag? Let me explain.

We live in a world with many temptations that can easily draw us away from God. We can decide to put many things before God, such as money, lust, golf, hunting, work, gambling, and many other pleasures of this world. We make decisions each and every day that affect our personal character and integrity. We make many of these decisions without much thought as to how this will affect our relationship with God. Some of these decisions, though, do have a great impact on our character, our integrity, and which path we choose: heaven or hell.

Before we get to laser tag, let's define character and integrity and see what the Bible has to say about these values.

Character

The Google dictionary defines character as "the mental and moral qualities distinctive to an individual." This is a *good* definition of character. We would all agree that we want to raise our sons to become men of character. But we want to be *great* dads, right? To become great dads, we need to reference the Bible and seek God's advice on raising our sons to become men of godly character.

Look at what Paul has to say about character in Romans 5:3–4:

> ...but we also glory in our sufferings, because we know that suffering produces perseverance; perseverance, character; and character, hope.

We must teach our sons that life is not always easy, carefree, and without pain and suffering. God builds our character through our suffering. Sometimes suffering comes from making decisions that are difficult. Sometimes these decisions go against our friends', families', or teammates' beliefs. As Christians, we must inform our sons that God's way is always the right way, but it may often be the most challenging way. These decisions build character. These decisions keep you on the narrow path and away from the wide-open path to destruction.

The legendary coach, John Wooden, had this to say about character:

> *Be more concerned with your character than your reputation, because your character is what you really are, while your reputation is merely what others think you are.*[2]

Integrity

Integrity is defined as "the quality of being honest and having strong moral principles: moral uprightness." I think C.S. Lewis defines integrity best: "doing the right thing even when no one is watching."[3] I personally believe that integrity should be the leadoff hitter of how to live your life God's way. For them to become men of integrity, we must teach our sons to aim small and miss small in everything that life throws at them. Whether it be a fastball, curveball, knuckleball, or slider, the devil has perfected them all and will throw us any pitch he thinks we will swing at in order to move us away from God.

Integrity is a value of the heart and comes from within each of us. With the gift of integrity, God gives us the responsibility to lead others to be men of integrity, including our sons. Psalm 78:72 reinforces this responsibility: "And David shepherded them with the integrity of the heart, with skillful hands he led them." The devil deters us from leading ourselves and our sons to lives of integrity. He tries and often succeeds.

In Titus, Paul writes, "in everything, set them an example by doing what is good. In your teaching show integrity, seriousness, and soundness of speech" (Titus 2:7–8). During today's Game Day, set an expectation for your son by being the example of integrity, seriousness, and soundness of speech.

Pre-Game Day Prayer

Dear Heavenly Father,

Tonight, _____ (your son's name) and I are beginning our 10-game journey toward not only a better father and son relationship but also toward a closer relationship with you! We thank you for this focused and intentional time together as we learn to apply Your word from Matthew to our lives today. Please allow both _____ (your son's name) and I to learn what it means to be a man of character and integrity through Your eyes. We know that Matthew states that the gate and road to heaven is small and narrow. Help us to aim small and miss small in our decisions, thoughts, and actions so that we may enter the narrow gate and become one of the few that "find it." In Jesus' name we pray, Amen.

Playbook

1. Pick a day that you and your son can spend at least one hour together at the local laser tag arena.
2. Before you drive to the laser tag arena, have your son read Matthew 7:13–14. Review the story from *The Patriot* and the lesson of "aim small, miss small."
3. Review the definitions of character and integrity with your son. It's all right to read right from this book.
4. Play at least one game of laser tag.

5. If possible, choose a laser tag name like "Integrity4God" or "Character Counts." Be creative and purposeful!

6. Focus on how challenging it is to aim your laser at your opponents' target vest sensors.

7. After the game, review your shooting statistics: shots fired, shots hit, hit percentage, and, of course, total score. You will use this in your Post-Game Day Analysis.

8. Find a spot where you and your son can grab a soda and snack for your Post-Game Day Analysis.

Audible Options

For those of you that do not have laser tag as an option, here are a couple of other ideas that will bring home the point of Game Day #1:

a) Darts (either at home or at a local establishment)

b) Mini-golf

c) Shooting or archery range (only if you and your son have taken the proper gun and/or archery safety classes!)

d) Any type of activity that requires a small target or goal will do!

Post-Game Day Analysis

We know that we learn more if we analyze our past performances. We also know that pee-wee athletes to professional athletes review and analyze their performances after the game to see how they can improve for the next game. Let's look at how you and your son performed at laser tag today.

After reviewing the stats and standings, ask your son the following questions:

1. Why do you think you had so many more shots fired than targets hit?
2. Why was your shot percentage _____%?
3. Did you always "aim small and miss small" when you pulled the trigger? Or did you fire randomly without thinking or aiming and hope to hit someone by luck or by chance?
4. What if you were to think of every shot fired as a decision that you have made in your life? Do you make decisions in life without thinking before you make them?
5. What are some examples of decisions you have made without thinking? How did those decisions turn out, and how did you feel about them?
6. How do you think God wants us to make decisions? Does God want us to make decisions before we really think about them? Or does God want us to make decisions out of love and respect for Him and for others?
7. Can you think of a time when you thought about your decision before you made it—with God and others in mind? How did that decision make you feel?

Dads, be prepared to share some of your own decisions. Once you get talking, your son will likely have questions for you. I would also suggest sharing some of the other Bible verses scattered throughout this chapter to help you build the integrity and character of your son.

Once you feel you and your son have fully analyzed the laser tag game, it is now time to get out your smartphone camera or video camera for the Post-Game Day Press Conference! I have prepared a few media questions for each of you to answer on camera. You can do this wherever you choose: at the table where you did your Post-Game Day Analysis, in the car (parking lot or your driveway), at home, or wherever else you choose.

Post-Game Day Press Conference

<u>Media Questions for Dad:</u>

Have your son start recording and ask you the following questions:

1. First things first, Dad...who won at laser tag?
2. Dad, what was your favorite part about today?
3. Dad, did you memorize Matthew 7:13–14? If so, can you say it now?
4. Dad, can you tell me about a time when you were proud of me for showing character or integrity?

<u>Media Questions for Son:</u>

Start filming, and ask your son the following questions:

1. _____ (Your son's name), what was your favorite part about today?
2. What was one thing that you learned about integrity and character today?
3. In the Bible, Titus tells us to set an example by doing good. Tell me about a time when you did something good for others and set an example for others to follow.
4. How would you rate today's Game Day? Circle the bullseyes below: (1 = Not so good and 5 = Awesome)

🎯🎯🎯🎯🎯

Dads, I would encourage you to save this video on your computer with the intent of compiling all of the videos at the end of the season for you to watch together to see how far both of you have come in your walk with God! I would also like you to consider sharing your Post-Game Day Press Conference videos on Facebook at the Friday Night Lights for Fathers and Sons Facebook page. Sharing your videos will provide other dads with even more fun and creative ways to spend time with their sons.

Link's X's and O's

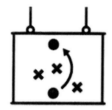

X: I loved playing laser tag with my dad! I can't wait until our next Game Day!
O: I have heard my dad talk about integrity before, and now I know that it's in the Bible.

Post-Game Day Prayer

Heavenly Father, _____ (your son's name) and I would like to thank You for the time we had together today. We thank You for not only the fun we had together but for the focused time we had learning about how You want us to live our lives with integrity and character. May we work hard to aim small and miss small in our decisions and our actions and to look to You and Your word when we need help. Help us to set an example for other dads and sons of how You created us to be. We pray that You help us find time not only for the next Game Day but for the rest of the games as well.
In Jesus' name we pray, Amen.

Well, dads and sons, congratulations! You have completed the first game of your 10-game season. Turn the page to get a sneak peek at the next Game Day! See you soon.

> *A righteous man who walks in his integrity—*
> *How blessed are his sons after him*
> — PROVERBS 20:7 (NASB)

GAME DAY 2

"Show Me the Money"

What does the Bible say about work and money?

Game Plan

Game Day Theme: Work and Money

God's Key Play: Matthew 25:29

Game Day Activity: Talent Search

God's Key Play

For whoever has will be given more, and they will
have an abundance. Whoever does not have, even
what they have will be taken from them.
— MATTHEW 25:29

Scouting Report for Dads

In high school, his dad gave him a book on investing. He read it in a weekend and asked his dad to help him open up an IRA (Individual Retirement Account). His dad complied, and soon the high schooler's dad made an everlasting effect on his son and his son's future family. Over the next few weeks, the dad and son talked about everything from stocks and bonds to commission rates and capital. However, the one definition that made the most impact was *compound interest*. The dad, never having been taught about this term prior to reading this book, shared one of the wisest lessons in investments. The son continued to work during high school and college, including summer vacations. He worked because his dad worked. He worked because his dad modeled a work ethic that inspired him to be the best at whatever job he was doing. He worked because he wanted his dad to be proud of him for working.

Each month, he continued to respect compound interest and knew that the money would someday not only benefit him but his future family as well. In fact, during a few challenging months, his dad covered the money so he could continue to invest. When he was able, the son paid him back in full—with interest!

I treasure several lessons from this story, namely that this dad purposely provided his son with a book on investing for his future; something the dad most certainly wished he could have done for himself at his son's young age. He also shared the power of compound interest. The dad in this story continued to support his son during the few months when the son was unable to invest. But most importantly, the dad modeled a strong work ethic for his son to follow.

Does this sound like a dad you would want to have? Does this sound like the dad you had? Or does this sound like the dad you would like to be? Perhaps you already are like the dad in this story.

Would you like to hear more about this dad?

As you might expect, the son went on to complete a four-year degree and earned a modest salary right after graduation. His dad, as he had for the past decade or so, worked one extra shift per week to pay for the fun things in life. His dad continued to talk highly of his job, the people he helped, and the people he worked with. With or without knowing it, this dad taught his son the importance of loving the work you do. The son continued to learn his trade, was accepted into a highly competitive internship, and was soon working exactly where he wanted to be!

The son soon was married and started a family of his own. He and his wife both worked full time and began paying back their student loans. They planned on aggressively paying off their debt. However, as life has a way of sidetracking all of us, they bought a home on a 30-year mortgage, furniture to fill the house, a brand new car, baby clothes, toys, and diapers! Within a couple of years, the young family was now in debt—to the tune of around $180,000, mortgage included! The son never asked his dad for any help. The dad never offered any help. The son and his wife had done this on their own, much like many other young couples that borrow money to pay for a college education and decide to buy a home soon after college.

One day, the couple had finally had enough. They were disappointed in the debt they had accumulated. They became more intentional about their finances. They were taught that the Bible is the best investment book on the market, and they began to understand that God doesn't want us to have debt but rather wants us to be successful and wants us to give to those not as fortunate.

Nearly six years to the day that they had called out their debt, this couple, along with their children, yelled, "We're debt free!" at the top of their lungs, live on *The Dave Ramsey Show*. The couple, not yet 40, with two tween children, had no mortgage, no car payments, and no debt at all!

The couple decided to share their story of sacrifice and success with the son's mom and dad during brunch at a fancy restaurant. Guess who paid?

The son's parents were proud of what their son and daughter-in-law had accomplished. The son had always remembered the value of investing by sacrificing a small amount of money each month as a direct result of the lesson his dad taught him that weekend in high school. On the day he learned of his son's accomplishment, he smiled brighter, hugged tighter, walked taller, and knew that he had succeeded as a father.

Head Fake

Now it's time for the head fake! This is the story of my dad and I. I will be forever grateful to my dad for sharing his investment book with me, for leading by example, and for believing in me. Both my dad and I would agree that we have made many mistakes, but this was not one of them. My dad didn't even know that my wife and I were actively trying to pay off all of our debt; however, the seed that he planted in my mind back when I was in high school, his work ethic, and his unconditional love made all the difference in the world.

For those of you that are interested, you can check out my family's Debt Free Scream on *The Dave Ramsey Show* on my website, marklamaster.com

Pre-Game Planning

I shared the story of how my dad taught me about money not to boast but to show a real-life example of the impact we can have on our sons—how providing our sons with one simple lesson can have an everlasting effect on their lives and beyond.

Money

If you haven't heard of Dave Ramsey, stop reading this book now and go buy his book, *The Total Money Makeover*. If you haven't taken Dave Ramsey's Financial Peace University (FPU), sign up soon! Jen and I first took FPU online. We loved it so much that we took it at our church the next year. Ever since, we have been FPU small group leaders. Recently, Dave and his daughter, Rachel Cruze, co-authored *Smart Money, Smart Kids*, which is also a wonderful reference for teaching your son about money!

Full disclosure: I am not a financial expert. But I have learned how to manage my money God's way with the guidance and inspiration of Dave Ramsey and his team. Dave taught me that God has given us more than 800 scriptures showing us how to handle money His way![1] Dave piqued my interest with this comment, and I had to look into this a little deeper.

Here is what I found. In his book, *The Treasure Principle*, Randy Alcorn provides many pearls of wisdom regarding God's perspective on money and our relationship with Him:

> Throughout the Bible there are roughly 2,350 verses concerning money. This is roughly twice as many as faith and prayer combined. Fifteen percent of everything Jesus said related to money and possessions. He spoke about money and possessions more than heaven and hell combined. The only subject Jesus spoke of more often is the Kingdom of God. Why? Because the Scriptures make clear there is a fundamental connection between a person's spiritual life and his attitudes and actions concerning money and possessions. Often we divorce the two—Christ sees them as essentially related to one another.[2]

You see, after reading so many "how-to" books on investing, Dave Ramsey's plan showed me that the Bible contains everything I need to know about managing my money. We need to teach our sons that God provides us with everything we need to know about this subject.

Work

Our sons also need to know that God wants us to use the blessings He has given us for His glory. Each and every one of us has a God-given talent:

> *We have different gifts, according to the grace given us.*
> *If a man's gift is prophesying, let him use it in proportion*
> *to his faith. If it is serving, let him serve; if it is teaching,*
> *let him teach; if it is encouraging, let him encourage;*
> *if it is contributing to the needs of others, let him give*
> *generously; if it is leadership, let him govern diligently;*
> *if it is showing mercy, let him do it cheerfully.*
> — ROMANS 12:6–8

As dads, we have the responsibility to guide our sons toward their God-given gift. Proverbs 22:6 tells us to "Train up a child in the way he should go, and he will not depart from it." As I said in the introduction, when I first heard Robert Lewis recite Proverbs 22:6, I had been a dad on a mission to become the dad God wanted me to become. My hope is that either this verse or one of the verses in this book becomes the verse that ignites your passion to become the dad God wants you to become.

Let's take a brief moment to consider the talents God has given your son. To help get you started, I will share some of the talents God has given to my son, Lincoln:

1. A caring, considerate, and compassionate heart
2. A mechanical and analytical mind (not passed on from his father!)
3. Athletic ability and hand–eye coordination
4. A knack for reading comprehension
5. A quick and witty sense of humor

Now take some time to list at least five talents God has gifted to your son. It may be easy for some of you and a bit of a challenge for others. This will be helpful during your Game Day activity!

1. _____
2. _____
3. _____
4. _____
5. _____

Now would also be a good time to consider five talents that God has gifted to you! Your son will ask—it will be better to be prepared than to be stumbling or speechless!

1. _____
2. _____
3. _____
4. _____
5. _____

Honestly, which one was easier to list out? This would be a great discussion to have with your son. Oftentimes it is much easier to list out others' talents than your own. Teach your son to know and take pride in his talents.

Before we have completed our Pre-Game Planning, let's talk about our own work and how it impacts how our sons perceive work. At the beginning of this chapter, I shared the story about how my dad modeled a strong work ethic, even working extra shifts for the fun stuff. What I did not mention is that I never once heard my dad complain about work, at least not when I was within earshot. I wish I could say the same for myself. In fact, when I asked Lincoln if he has ever heard me complain about work, he said, "Yeah, at least every week or two." Really? This made me take a step back and contemplate how this was impacting his view on work.

In their book, *Smart Money, Smart Kids*, Ramsey and Cruze state that "You should view teaching your children to work in the same way you view teaching them to bathe and brush their teeth—as a necessary skill for life."[3] Ramsey and Cruze also discuss the learning concept in which "more is caught than taught."[4] Do you think

Lincoln has a positive image of work when I come home once every week or two and complain about it? What has your son "caught" from you about work?

Well, there we have it; God clearly cares about how we handle our money and provides us with up to 2,350 verses on the subject in the Bible. He also directs us to train our sons up in the talents He has blessed them with. Now it's time for our Game Day activity!

You have made it to Game 2 of the season and have learned a great deal about what the Bible says about work and money. How often, if ever, has your son seen you at your workplace, especially in your work clothes? Make the extra effort to arrange this activity at your work. It might take a bit of time and a few phone calls, but your son will greatly appreciate it!

Our money is not ours! It is for God's Kingdom! We just have the privilege of managing it for a while. What will you and your son do with the money you are blessed with?

Pre-Game Day Prayer

Dear Heavenly Father,

Work and money are deeply tied to a man's mind. As _____ (your son's name) and I discuss these two topics today, please help us to remember that You have already given us everything we need in this life. Help us to look to Your Word for guidance on work and money. We pray that our time together today is focused and intentional but that we also become closer as father and son. I pray that _____ (your son's name) has a better understanding about the talents God has given him after our time together. I also pray that the lessons _____ (your son's name) learns today about work and money help to set a firm foundation upon which to build a strong understanding of what You have planned for him. I pray that I can purposely model a strong work ethic and biblical understanding of how to manage my money so that _____ (your son's name) is able to "catch" more than what is taught today. Thank You for the time that we have together.

In Jesus' name we pray, Amen.

Playbook

1. Materials you will need:
    a. Multiple bills in whatever denomination you choose
    b. Dress up in your work clothes (suit, business casual, scrubs, uniform, etc.)
    c. Bible with Mathew 25:14–30 bookmarked
    d. The list you made about your son's talents
    e. Pen and paper/notepad
    f. Smartphone or video camera
    g. FNL4FS book

2. Location options:
    Your work location (office, work site, building lobby, or conference room)—make sure that you have permission to use the area you choose. After hours may work for some of you that do not work in 24/7 roles.

3. At the location you choose, inform your son that he has just signed a contract to play quarterback for his favorite pro football team. The money spread out on the table represents his signing bonus. (A conference room table or your office desk would work great!)

4. Ask your son how he will spend the money when you give it to him. Take out your pen and paper and write down his answers.
    a. Dave Ramsey recommends that we split our earnings into three separate categories: Spend (80%), Save (10%), and Give (10%).[5]

    b.   Make sure you and your son discuss his answers in detail, and be prepared to answer the same question from your son about your finances.

5.   Game Changer:

Now ask your son the following hypothetical question: What if the contract stated that you may take the signing bonus money ($1,000) now but had to return every penny of it exactly one year from today? Then ask your son what he would do with the money.

    a.   Write down his answers, and answer any follow-up questions he may have.

    b.   Once you have discussed this in detail, tell him the following story:

Jesus once told a very similar story about three guys who were asked a very similar question—it was obviously not about signing a pro football contract, but hang with me. Before the boss of these three guys went on a long trip, he gave each of them a different amount of money. Each one of these guys had to make a very important decision on what to do with the money their boss gave them. Do you think they spent it? Do you think they wasted it? What do you think they did with it? Well, let's find out.

6.   Open your Bible to Matthew 25:14–30 (Parable of the Talents)

    a.   Explain that a talent is a unit of money (like the dollar)—well, a lot of money. A talent was worth about 20 years of wages at the time.[6]

    b.   Begin reading the passage. While you are doing this, hand out money to your son.

Audible Options

For those of you that are unable to arrange time at your work location, here are a couple of other ideas that will work just as well:

1. Bank lobby
2. A friend or family member's office or conference room
3. Private or secluded table at a local restaurant
4. Picnic table or park bench (weather permitting)
5. Kitchen table

Make sure you dress up in your work clothes regardless of your location.

Post-Game Day Analysis

Now let's dig deeper into what Jesus wanted us to learn from this passage in Matthew, also called the Parable of the Talents. This is where you can truly coach your son to look at money and work just as God wants us to.

1. _____ (Your son's name), when I talk about work and money, does it make you happy or sad? (His answer may surprise you. Take the time now to discuss this important question).
2. How much was each servant given, and what did he do with the money?
3. In the Parable of the Talents, how did the master respond to the two servants who returned more money than they were given?
4. Which servant made the master angry, and what was his punishment?
5. What do you think Jesus' lesson was in telling this parable?
6. Who else is given multiple talents, blessings, and money and is expected to use them the way God intended? (This is the perfect time

to reiterate your son's blessings, his work ethic, and how God wants him to use his blessings and future earnings.)

It is now time to get out your smartphone or video camera for the Post-Game Day Press Conference! I have prepared a few media questions for each of you to answer on camera.

Post-Game Day Press Conference

Media Questions for Your Son:

Start recording, and ask your son the following questions:

1. What is the most important thing you learned about money today?
2. What is the most important thing you learned about work today?
3. Tell me a little bit about what you were thinking when I told you that our money is actually God's money?
4. What was your favorite part about today's Game Day?
5. How would you rate today's Game Day? Circle the dollar signs below (1= Not so good, and 5 = Awesome)

Media Questions for Dad:

Have your son start recording and have him ask you the following questions:

1. When did you get your first job, and how much did you make per hour?
2. Dad, did you manage your money well when you were a kid?

3. Dad, if you could change jobs, what would you do and why?
4. What was your favorite part about today?

Just a quick reminder to share your videos with other dads and sons via the Friday Night Lights for Fathers and Sons Facebook page.

Link's X's and O's

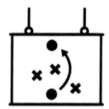

X: It was fun hanging out where my dad works. I want to have an office like his some day.
O: I thought it was cool to learn that our family's money is actually God's money.

Post-Game Day Prayer

Dear Heavenly Father,

We know that You created men to do Your work and to do it all for the glory of God (1 Corinthians 10:31). We also know that we are to be stewards of Your money. _____ (Your son's name) and I have learned so much together today and pray that You continually guide us to use the talents You have blessed us with to improve and expand Your Kingdom. Help me to be the best dad that I can be, and guide me to raise _____(your son's name) to know You. I also pray that You help me to identify and nurture the talents you have given him. We thank You for the precious time we had together today and pray that we continue to grow closer in our relationship with You.

In Jesus' name we pray, Amen.

> *So whether you eat or drink or whatever*
> *you do, do it all for the glory of God.*
> — 1 CORINTHIANS 10:31

GAME DAY 3*

The Best Offense Is a Good Defense

Defend your son from the Internet, pornography, and video game addiction.

Game Plan

Game Day Theme: The Internet, pornography, and video game addiction

God's Key Play: Romans 12:2

Game Day Activity: Bookstore and Arcade

God's Key Play

*Do not conform to the pattern of this world, but be
transformed by the renewing of your mind. Then
you will be able to test and approve what God's
will is—His good, pleasing and perfect will.*
— ROMANS 12:2

Scouting Report for Dads

*Special Note: Today's Game Day gets extremely personal and may not be age appropriate for your son. Please review the material. If you have not had the "S-E-X Talk" with your son, you may want to consider having it soon. Please read this entire chapter and decide whether or not it is appropriate for your son.

Andrew Fulton flunked out of college and lost 30 pounds, and it wasn't because he was partying. It wasn't because he didn't have loving parents. It wasn't because he wasn't successful in high school—in fact, he was a "good kid," an honors student, and a talented musician. Fulton flunked out of college because of an addiction—an addiction to the Internet and gaming.[1]

In a 2014 segment on *The Today Show*, Fulton shared that he spent an average of six hours per day online. While in college, he would spend 12–16 hours a day/night playing online games and surfing the Internet. He would eat a piece of bread and cheese then would keep on playing and surfing.[1]

When asked why he spent so much time online, he said it was to escape all of his stressors. "It's really like a therapeutic release. All that social anxiety I felt in school just went away because I could be whoever I wanted to be...it's kind of like a full-body buzz."[1]

John was 10 years old and decided to check college football scores on the Internet. On the bottom right-hand corner of the website, John saw a nearly naked woman and clicked on the picture without thinking twice. Before he knew it, he was watching his first porn clip. It made him a bit uncomfortable but excited as well. Soon he was watching at least 75 porn clips per week. His parents had no idea. He just told them he was working on homework.

Fast forward 15 years...John became engaged to his college sweetheart, the love of his life. He had not kicked the porn habit despite multiple attempts. When his fiancée found out, she began to lose trust in him. Unfortunately, porn's grip on John was more powerful than the love he had for his fiancée. His fiancée canceled their wedding plans.

Unfortunately, John and Andrew's stories are not uncommon. So what's fueling stories like Andrew's, John's, and those of other young men as they attempt to escape real life? Psychologist Philip Zimbardo, Ph.D., past president of the American Psychological Association and a professor emeritus at Stanford, fired off the following facts during his 2011 TED (Technology, Entertainment, and Design) Talk entitled "The Demise of Guys":

> What are the causes? Well, it's an unintended consequence. I think its excessive Internet use in general, excessive video gaming, excessive new access to pornography. The problem is these are arousal addictions. Drug addiction, you simply want more. Arousal addiction, you want different. Drugs, you want more of the same—different. So you need the novelty in order for the arousal to be sustained.
>
> And the problem is the industry is supplying it. Jane McGonigal told us last year that by the time a boy is 21, he's played 10,000 hours of video games, most of that in isolation. As you remember, Cindy Gallop said men don't know the difference between making love and doing porn. The average boy now watches 50 porn video clips a week...and the porn industry is the fastest growing industry in America—$15 billion annually. For every 400 movies made in Hollywood, there are now 11,000 porn videos made.[2]

Houston, I think we have a problem. Zimbardo's research is legit. His research is based off a survey of 20,000 people and how they interact with porn and gaming.[3] Dads, did you guys know Internet, porn, and gaming were such an issue in our country? Here are some titles from recent books and blogs about the addictive powers of Internet, porn, and gaming:

Books

- *Unplugged: My Journey into the Dark World of Video Game Addiction*[4]
- *Your Brain on Porn: Internet Porn and the Emerging Science of Addiction*[5]
- *The Demise of Guys: Why Boys Are Struggling and What We Can Do About It*[3]
- *PlayStation Nation: Protect Your Child from Video Game Addiction*[6]
- *Cyber Junkie: Escape the Gaming and Internet Trap*[7]

Blogs

- Teens and Porn: 10 Stats You Need to Know[8]
- Effects of Porn on Adolescent Boys[9]
- These Two Traps Are Absolutely Destroying the Next Generation of Young Men In America[10]
- Hooked! The Addictive Power of Video Games[11]

Here are some additional statistics that will shock you:

- 70% of boys have spent more than 30 consecutive minutes looking at online porn on at least one occasion; 35% of these boys have done this on more than 10 occasions.
- 83% of boys have seen group sex on the Internet.
- 69% of boys have seen porn showing same-sex intercourse.
- 39% of boys have seen online sex acts involving bondage.
- 32% of boys have viewed bestiality on the Internet.

- 18% of boys have seen rape or sexual violence online.
- 15% of boys have seen child pornography.[12]

Perhaps the most shocking statistic to me is that 93% of boys see porn before the age of 18![12]

I don't know about you, but these statistics make me sick to my stomach or feel like I just got punched in the gut.

Research has shown that addiction to the Internet, porn, and gaming release high levels of dopamine. The problem is real. It's time to play some defense against one of the devil's greatest games against our sons. Let's take a look at what defensive strategies we dads can implement. Can you guess what one of the best references is? You guessed it! The Bible.

Pre-Game Planning

Before we can play defense for our sons, we have to evaluate our own game plan. In a recent study by the Barna Group, 64% of Christian men admitted to viewing pornography at least once a month.[13] That means at least six out of ten dads reading this book watch porn themselves!

If you are one of these six dads, you must address this issue internally—now! For those of you that feel that you are so far lost in porn that you can't possibly find your way out, there is help! One of the best moves you can make is to automatically track your web viewing and to have an accountability partner or two.

One of the best ways that I know of how to resist the temptations of the grip of pornography is a software program called Covenant Eyes, founded by Ron DeHaas. The mission of Covenant Eyes is to "equip people with tools that provide protection and encourage accountability and trust in the fight against Internet temptation."[14]

As a Christian, DeHaas became concerned about what his two teenage sons were viewing on the Internet. His curiosity concluded in the creation of Covenant Eyes. Covenant Eyes is a software program that can provide Internet accountability and Internet filtering for you and your family.

Covenant Eyes provides a report of your child's Internet viewing as well as offering the option for you to enlist friends as your own accountability partners. There are certainly other Internet filtering programs available, but I prefer Covenant Eyes because it was built by a dad who was concerned about his sons' future. DeHaas had the vision that by helping his own sons, he could influence and impact the lives of millions of others. He is doing God's work every day of his life. If you want to find out more about Covenant Eyes, check them out at covenanteyes.com.

Before we move on to the Playbook, I want to offer up a challenge for you and your son. The original challenge comes from the book of Job. It goes like this:

I made a covenant with my eyes not to look lustfully at a young woman (Job 31:1)

So, you might say, Job lived 2,500 years ago, how could this possibly be relevant today? For starters, Ron DeHaas developed an Internet accountability software program based on this verse, Covenant Eyes. In addition, Stephen Arterburn and Fred Stoeker wrote a book about it: *Every Young Man's Battle: Strategies for Victory in the Real World of Sexual Temptation.*

Arterburn and Stoeker offer up a Job challenge for all of us Christian men; they call it "bouncing the eyes": "When your eyes bounce toward a woman's attributes, they must bounce away immediately."[15]

As part of your Pre-Game Planning, I challenge you to make a covenant with your eyes not to look lustfully at not only women other than your wife but to also add video games and endless Internet searching to your list.

For the purposes of FNL4FS, I would like to add a couple of layers to this challenge.

- When your eyes bounce toward a woman's attributes in person or online, they must bounce away immediately.
- Once you have set appropriate limits for Internet and gaming, bounce your eyes away immediately.
- Enlist the help of a friend, family member, or teammate to become your online accountability partner.

This is a tough challenge, but I think you are up to it. You and your son's eternity could depend on it.

Pre-Game Day Prayer

Dear Heavenly Father,

We know that during today's Game Day, we will be answering some tough questions. We know that You already know what's in our hearts and minds, but sometimes it is difficult to share secrets with those that are closest to us. Help us to be honest in our answers today. We have learned that Satan likes to distract us and to confuse us in this life to keep us from knowing You better. Your Word says that we should not conform to the ways of this world but to look to Your Word to transform and renew our minds. Guide us through the traps that Satan has set for us, and help us to focus our eyes on You.
In Jesus' name we pray, Amen.

Playbook

Before I go on with the Playbook for today's Game Day, I have a confession to make. This was the hardest Game Day for me to write. It was incredibly irritating to write for the following reasons:

- Multiple distractions
- Lack of focus and clarity
- Computer and Internet issues
- A sense of fear in sharing this information
- Multiple other emotions that were constantly confusing

I literally sat down to write this Game Day at least a dozen times without completion. There was just something about this topic that made me feel like I should not continue with my research and writing. As I did every other time I sat down to write, I would pray to God and the Holy Spirit for guidance and clarity in the choice of my words so that they would resonate with fathers everywhere.

I have come to the conclusion that all of these distractions are the resistance of the evil one. Once I was able to identify this, I was able to pray more effectively and was eventually able to complete this Game Day.

I write this not for you to feel sorry for me but to make you aware that today's Game Day may involve resistance. You may want to put this Game Day off because it is uncomfortable, awkward, not the right time, or for a variety of other reasons. I encourage you to go forward with this Game Day and pray that you can fend off the devil's resistance.

Why? Because before your son gets married, Satan does everything he can to get him to have sex with his girlfriend; after he gets married, he does everything he can to keep him from having sex with his wife.[15]

All right, let's get ready for Game Day!

For today's Game Day, you will be hanging out in a local bookstore and arcade.

1. Materials needed
    a. FNL4FS book
    b. Pen or pencil
    c. Smartphone or video camera
    d. Bible

2. Location options:
    a. Bookstore such as Barnes and Noble, Books-a-Million, or a locally owned bookstore
    b. Video game arcade such as Chuck E. Cheese's or Dave and Buster's

3. Once you have decided what bookstore and video game arcade locations you will be visiting, sit in the car and ask your son the following questions:

    -   How many hours do you spend on the Internet per week?
    -   How many hours do you spend playing video games each week?
    -   Ask him if he knows what porn or pornography is. Whether he answers yes or no, just make a mental note of what his answer is, and we will explain more of it later on.
    -   Have you ever been tempted to click on Internet sites with women dressed in bikinis or other skimpy, revealing outfits?
    -   If so, how does this make you feel?
    -   Do you feel that you spend too much time on the Internet or playing video games? Why or why not?
    -   Have you or your friends ever looked at a *Playboy*, *Penthouse*, or other pornographic magazines?

4. Drive to the bookstore that you chose, and head to the magazine section. Locate the adult magazine section.

    a.   Ask you son why he thinks these types of magazines are sealed in a plastic wrap that blocks the images of the front cover.

    b.   If your son said no to the question above about having ever looked at adult magazines, explain to him why they are covered. Proceed to explain to him that this is to protect kids his age and up until 18 from the harmful effects of pornography.

    c.   If your son answered yes to the question about looking at porn magazines above, ask him if he would feel comfortable reading the same magazine in the store. Most likely he will say no. When he says no, ask him why he wouldn't feel comfortable. Explore this by asking follow-up questions that relate to how God views him looking at these types of magazines.

    d.   Read Job 31:1 to your son. Tell him about how you deal with the temptation of looking at beautiful women, adult magazines, and Internet porn.

    e.   Define and discuss pornography with your son. Inform him that pornography is one of the devil's best tools to distract boys and young men from living a Christian lifestyle. Share the story of John from the beginning of this chapter. Be prepared to give any examples of how you have personally dealt with porn from your past.

    f.   Before you leave the bookstore, make sure you have answered all of your son's questions and have made it clear that pornography is the work of the devil.

    g.   Statistical Analysis
- 93% of boys will see porn before the age of 18.
- Tell your son that you want to protect him from the dangers of pornography because more than 9 out of 10 boys will watch it before they are 18.

5. After your trip to the bookstore, tell your son that the next stop is the video arcade.
   a. Establish a monetary amount that you will be giving him to play with. When the tokens are spent, you will stop and get a snack and talk about the Game Day.
   b. Your son will likely ask for more money. If he does, tell him no and explain to him that there is a reason he wants to play more.

6. Grab a snack and a table or booth, and get ready to discuss how video games can become addictive.
   a. Statistical Analysis
      - By the age of 21, the average male will have played 10,000 hours of video games.
   b. Ask your son if he feels 10,000 hours of video games is how God wants him to spend his time.
   c. Tell your son that video games are intentionally designed for addiction. Olivia and Kurt Bruner, authors of *PlayStation Nation: Protect Your Child From Video Game Addiction*, list seven driving forces behind video game design:
      - Beating the Game
      - Competition
      - Mastery
      - Exploration
      - The High Score
      - Story-Driven Role Play
      - Relationships[6]
   d. Instead of the typical three "lives" for a token at the video arcade, home video console games have unlimited lives and the ability to save games as you advance to new levels or worlds.

Before we end this portion of today's Game Day, read today's God's Key Play out loud—twice.

> *Do not conform to the pattern of this world, but be*
> *transformed by the renewing of your mind. Then*
> *you will be able to test and approve what God's*
> *will is—his good, pleasing and perfect will.*
> — ROMANS 12:2

Explain the meaning of this verse to your son. Just because "everyone else is doing it" (Internet, porn, and gaming) does not mean that we need to. God wants us to be transformed by the purity of His perfect will!

I will admit, this Game Day was a challenge for Lincoln and I as well. But this is where our relationship grows and our faith in God begins to stretch! Now it's time for our Post-Game Analysis!

Post-Game Day Analysis

Here are some more questions to analyze how today's Game Day went.

1. Dad, have you ever watched porn online? Or, Dad, have you ever looked at adult magazines? If so, why?
2. _____ (Your son's name), how did you feel about the discussions about the Internet, pornography, and gaming today?
3. _____ (Your son's name), do any of your friends pressure you to watch porn on the Internet or play more games than you want to?
4. Why do you think Satan wants us to become addicted to the Internet, porn, and gaming?
5. How do you think God would want us to spend our time instead of searching the Internet, watching porn, or playing video games?

6. _____ (Your son's name), do you feel that you are addicted to the Internet, porn, or playing video games? (If your son answers yes to any of these, I would refer you to your family physician for further guidance.)
7. Review and commit to joining the "Bouncing the Eyes" challenge.

Post-Game Day Press Conference

Media Questions for Dad:

Have your son start recording and ask you the following questions:

1. Dad, do you worry about me becoming addicted to the things we talked about today?
2. Dad, what was your favorite video game when you were a kid? Why?
3. Dad, did you have a video game system when you were growing up? Which one?
4. What is Covenant Eyes, and when are we going to put this on our computer?
5. What was the most important thing you learned during today's Game Day?

Media Questions for Son:

Start filming, and ask your son the following questions:

1. _____ (Your son's name), what do you feel is the most important thing you learned from today's Game Day?
2. How do you think you will use what you learned today to make better use of the time God has blessed you with?
3. Do you think you can commit to the "Bouncing the Eyes" challenge?

4. Do you think that any of the video games you are playing today are not appropriate for you?

5. How would you rate today's Game Day? Circle the Pac-Mans below (1 Pac-Man = Not so good and 5 Pac-Mans = Awesome)

6. Tell your son you love him and that you will always be available to talk to him about anything!

Link's X's and O's

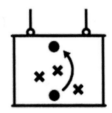

X: Now I know why my dad only lets me play video games for 30 minutes a day.

O: My dad taught me to bounce my eyes away from the Internet ads that I see when I look up sports scores.

Post-Game Day Prayer

Dear Heavenly Father,

_____ (Your son's name) and I thank You for the time we were able to spend together today. We have learned much, not only about each other but also about Your enduring love and Your strategies against the evil one, Satan. It is so easy to get caught up in the addictive things of this life—like the Internet, pornography, and gaming. Although the majority of Christian men and boys fall into these traps, we have learned that by looking to Your Word, we should not only avoid these traps but we should stand up and help others avoid them as well. Holy Spirit, continue to guide us to become more like You in our thoughts, minds, and souls so that we may be a beacon for Your purpose here on earth.

In Jesus' name we pray, Amen.

> *I made a covenant with my eyes not to*
> *look lustfully at a young woman.*
> — JOB 31:1

GAME DAY 4

How to Teach Your Son the Hail Mary— and I Don't Mean Doug Flutie's Pass

We must teach our sons the power of prayer in their lives.

Game Plan

Game Day Theme: Prayer

God's Key Play: James 5:16

Game Day Activity: Playing catch with your son

God's Key Play

*Therefore confess your sins to each other and pray
for each other so that you may be healed. The prayer
of a righteous person is powerful and effective.*
— JAMES 5:16

Scouting Report for Dads

The Ramblers were 4th and 6th on Tech's six-yard line. After three red zone running plays that resulted in only five yards, Noble Kizer kneeled down in the huddle and said, "Boys, let's have us a Hail Mary." The Ramblers recited the Hail Mary prayer as they huddled around their star quarterback, Elmer Layden. On the next play, Layden threw a touchdown pass to put the Ramblers ahead of Tech, 7–3. In fact, on the next play, after another Tech muffed kick return, the Ramblers again found themselves in a third and goal situation. Kizer again said, "Let's have another Hail Mary." Again, Layden threw another touchdown pass.[1]

The Ramblers went on to beat Tech that day, but more importantly, the legend of the "Hail Mary Pass" was born. In fact, this game took place in 1922 between the Notre Dame Ramblers and Georgia Tech. The star quarterback for the now Notre Dame Fighting Irish in 1922, Elmer Layden, was one the Four Horsemen of Notre Dame coached by none other than Knute Rockne.[1] Ironically, Noble Kizer, the player who suggested the Hail Mary prayer, was a Presbyterian. Sorry to spoil it for those of you who thought the first Hail Mary Pass in football was Boston College's Doug Flutie's successful Hail Mary Pass to beat the University of Miami in 1984!

This story is not only a cool historical piece for us football fans but it also demonstrates that God doesn't differentiate between Catholics or Presbyterians and answers prayers even when they are related to sports—we just need to pray!

Being an avid college football fan, I cannot talk about Notre Dame football without somehow mentioning my favorite team, the Nebraska Cornhuskers. It just so happens that the Burpo family is from Nebraska, and I can almost guarantee that they are Nebraska Cornhusker fans!

If the name Burpo sounds familiar, it is most likely that you have heard of either the book or the movie by the same name, *Heaven Is for Real*. On a family trip, Colton (age 4) becomes gravely ill. After five days of not knowing the cause of the illness, his parents, Todd (a pastor) and Sonja, learn that Colton has suffered a ruptured appendix and must have emergency surgery.[2]

Despite Colton being clinically close to death both before and after the surgery, it is soon discovered that Colton has experienced heaven. Through conversations with his parents, Colton reveals his experiences in heaven and becomes the central message of the book.[2] The book went on to become a New York Times #1 Best Seller, and the movie was a box office success!

Not to take away from the heaven experience from the Burpos' story, but I want to focus on Todd Burpo's fight for his son's life. Even though Todd Burpo is a pastor, his faith is challenged as he witnesses his son's health deteriorate quickly over a few rocky days in the hospital. The power of prayer throughout *Heaven Is for Real* must not be overlooked. Instead, it should be recognized and modeled for all of us dads.

Let's take a look at a few of the examples of the power of prayer in *Heaven Is for Real*:

- Frustrated that he was not getting answers at the small-town hospital, Todd Burpo prayed, "He's getting worse, God! What do we do?" This prayer was quickly answered, and it was decided that they would transfer Colton to a larger hospital in North Platte, Nebraska.[2]
- Todd and Sonja had lost a daughter to miscarriage several years before. When Sonja learned that Colton might die, Todd imagined Sonja thinking, *What are you doing, God? Are you going to take this child too?*[2]
- Once alone in a private room, Todd Burpo had had enough! He slammed the door and began raging at God: "Where are you? Is this how you treat your pastors?! Is it even worth it to serve you?" Todd continued, "After the leg, the kidney stones, the mastectomy, this is how you're going to let me celebrate the end of my testing?...You're going to take my son?"[2]

- Todd and Sonja called family and friends to pray. Todd also called his secretary at the church to activate the prayer chain for Colton, citing that God also answers the prayers of the friends of the sick and dying.[2]
- During Colton's surgery, Todd and Sonja sat together and prayed.[2]
- After a successful surgery, Colton and his family were ready to be discharged from the hospital when the doctor gave them some bad news—Colton's condition was worsening, and he would need to be transferred to a metropolitan hospital that could provide more complex care. Unfortunately, due to a large winter storm, transporting Colton to another hospital was impossible.[2]
- Unbeknownst to the Burpos, at about this same time, 80 friends and family were assembling at the Burpos' church to pray for Colton. The next day, without being transferred to another hospital, Colton began to feel better![2]

These are just a few examples that illustrate the power of prayer. The Burpos have shown us that God hears us whether we pray alone with our heads bowed, pray together with others, seek the prayers of others, or yell out at Him in rage. Todd does not give up hope and keeps fighting for Colton. He knows that he has no control over the situation and that the only thing he can do is PRAY!

Have you experienced the power of prayer in your life? Have you had an experience with prayer as powerful as Todd Burpo, or has your experience with prayer been more like Notre Dame's Noble Kizer?

Two years ago, after attending the Global Leadership Summit, I was inspired by Bill Hybels to pray more often and to pray more intentionally. I bought his book, *Too Busy Not to Pray*, and was determined to develop my own prayer plan. I also began reading Stormie Omartian's *Power of a Praying* series, specifically *The Power of a Praying Parent* and *The Power of a Praying Husband*. I then stumbled upon a prayer journal idea from Lisa Whelchel, in which she designed to pray for multiple people each day in a strategic but effective way. Again, I love a good plan and guide to keep me on track and motivated!

I developed a prayer journal for my wife, Jen, and I to complete with plastic page covers and blank, college-ruled paper. Of course, I created my own because Jen and I did not want to spend the money during our debt-free journey!

I learned more about the power of prayer in that few weeks than I had in my entire life. As a dad and husband, I certainly prayed for my wife and kids, but it wasn't consistent, it wasn't intentional, and it was almost always to ask for something selfishly. My prayers rarely consisted of what Bill Hybels calls the A.C.T.S. approach to prayer:

- **A**doration
- **C**onfession
- **T**hanksgiving
- **S**upplication[3]

Stormie Omartian taught me that "our children's lives don't ever have to be left to chance."[4] Omartian goes on to say:

> The key is not trying to do it all by ourselves all at once, but rather turning to the expert parent of all time, our Father God, for help. Then, taking one step at a time, we must cover every detail of our child's life in prayer. There is great power in doing that, far beyond what most people imagine. In fact, don't ever underestimate the power of a praying parent.[4]

Dads, are you praying for your sons?

Pre-Game Planning

One of my favorite memories is playing catch with my dad. It didn't matter whether it was a football, a baseball, a Frisbee, a tennis ball, or even a wadded up piece of paper. I believe playing catch is one of the best ways to spend time with your son. Somehow, playing catch gets us guys in the mood to talk, whether it is about school, girls, work, sports, or religion. For today's Game Day, you will be tossing a football around with your son.

For those of you that do not have or do not want to throw a football, please see the Audible Options below for some alternative ideas.

Audible Options

1. For those of you who would rather play catch with a baseball or Frisbee, go for it!
2. Soccer fans, you can also pass the soccer ball back and forth for today's game.

Pre-Game Day Prayer

Dear Heavenly Father,

You are able to do all things! _____ (Your son's name) and I are amazed at Your power and strength. We realize that we sin every day, and we ask for Your forgiveness. Our hope is that our time together today not only strengthens our father and son relationship but also brings us closer to You. _____ (Your son's name) and I thank You for all that You have blessed us with and ask that You protect our family from any harm or health issues. Teach us to grow closer to You each and every day by establishing a daily prayer ritual. May the activities of today's game help us both to better understand the power of prayer.
In Jesus' name we pray, Amen.

Playbook

For today's Game Day, you will be reenacting the Hail Mary Pass play while playing catch at a local football field with your son.

1. Materials needed:
   a. Football (a size your son can grip and easily throw)
   b. FNL4FS book
   c. Smartphone or video camera
   d. Pen or pencil
2. Location options:
   Besides a local football field, you can choose a local park or gym. For the purposes of spending time with your son, I do encourage you to plan for somewhere other than your back yard.
3. Before you head out to the field with your son, have him read James 5:16.
4. On the way to the field, ask him the following questions:
   a. When was the last time you prayed to God?
   b. When was the last time you saw me praying?
5. Play catch for about 15 minutes. Catch up on your son's day, and let him know how yours was.
6. After about 15 minutes, throw your son a couple of good passes and then a couple of bad passes—passes that are easy to catch and passes that are way over his head and impossible to catch. Throw some passes with your non-dominant hand. Then throw some spiral passes and then some passes that are not.
7. By now, your son is most likely going to be wondering what you are doing. Remind him that there is a reason for what you are doing.
8. Game-changer: Find a seat on the bleachers or a park bench, and tell him why you were throwing the football all over the place.

a. Remind him that as humans, even though we may try our best, we live our lives "all over the place," just like some of the passes you threw to him. For a time, we can live the way God wants us to, but other times in our lives, we may drift and make bad decisions.

b. Next, ask your son if he thinks God could have caught those horrible passes.

c. Knowing that God could have caught all of those passes, ask him if he believes that God listens to and answers all of his prayers.

d. Share with him the quote that Bill Hybels shares about prayer: "If the request is wrong, God says, No. If the timing is wrong, God says, Slow. If you are wrong, God says, Grow. But if the request is right, the timing is right and you are right, God says, Go!"[3]

e. Remind your son that God indeed answers all prayers. Whether it is a perfect spiral or a knuckle ball, too high or too low, God has the power to do all things—you just need to pray.

f. Before you get into the Post-Game Day Analysis, reenact a successful Hail Mary Pass play.

Post-Game Day Analysis

One of my favorite country music songs is Rodney Atkins' "I've Been Watching You." If you haven't heard it, Atkins is singing about how his young son wants to be like him and copies everything that he does—anything from eating all of his food and fixing things to holding his momma's hand and wanting to grow as tall as he is. My favorite part is better left for Atkins to tell you:

We got back home and I went to the barn
I bowed my head and I prayed real hard
Said, "Lord, please help me help my stupid self."
Just this side of bedtime later that night
Turnin' on my son's Scooby-Doo nightlight.
He crawled out of bed and he got down on his knees.
He closed his little eyes, folded his little hands
Spoke to God like he was talkin' to a friend.
And I said, "Son, now where'd you learn to pray like that?"
He said, "I've been watching you, dad, ain't that cool?"[5]

Dads, our sons are watching us. Now it's time to dig a little deeper into today's Game Day and ask your son the following Post-Game Day Analysis questions.

1. How often do you pray to God?
2. How and when do you pray?
3. Can you tell me about a prayer of yours that God answered?
4. Can you tell me about a prayer of yours that you don't think God answered and why?
5. Would it help if I shared one way to pray with you?—Review the A.C.T.S. prayer template or the way in which you find it best to pray with your son.
6. If you do not currently pray with your child, ask your son if he would like you to pray with him each morning or each night. You might be surprised that he really wants you to!
7. If you don't currently pray for him, tell him that you will start as a result of today's Game Day. Please see the Fatherhood Personnel Files for a list of prayer books you can use for your son.

Get out your smartphone or video camera because it's now time for the Post-Game Day Presser!

Post-Game Day Press Conference

<u>Media Questions for Dad:</u>

Have your son start recording and ask you the following questions:

1. Dad, do you pray to God each day?
2. Dad, does God get mad at me when I don't pray to Him?
3. In James 5:16, James says that we should pray for others. Who all do you pray for?
4. Dad, will you promise to pray with me each night before I go to bed?
5. Dad, when you pray for me, what do you pray about?

<u>Media Questions for Son:</u>

Start filming, and ask your son the following questions:

1. _____ (Your son's name), what was your favorite part about today?
2. What was one thing that you learned about the power of prayer today?
3. Tell me about a time when you believe God answered your prayers.
4. How would you rate today's Game Day? Circle the footballs below (1 football = Not so good, and 5 footballs = Awesome).

Just a quick reminder to share your videos with other dads and sons via the Friday Night Lights for Fathers and Sons Facebook page.

Link's X's and O's

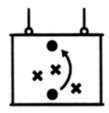

X: I try to pray every day, even though I do forget sometimes.
O: I learned to pray for others first, then for myself.

Post-Game Day Prayer

Dear Heavenly Father,

_____ (Your son's name) and I would like to thank You for the time we had together today. We thank You for not only the fun we had together but for the focused time we had learning about how we can grow closer to You through prayer. We learned that You answer all of our prayers in one way or another. Help us to always trust and understand that You can see the big picture in our lives and that a "No" to one of our prayers may be the best thing that ever happened to us. Finally, we pray that You help us find time not only for the next Game Day but for the rest of the games as well.
In Jesus' name we pray, Amen.

Well dads and sons, congratulations! You have completed the fourth game of the season. Get ready to get your hands dirty during Game Day 5!

*Dearest Jesus, through the night, love me, keep me,
hold me tight. Please keep me well and thank You for
everything, especially Jesus' love in my heart. Please help
the sad, the sick, and the lonely. Please teach the world
about love and not war. Please forgive my sins. Amen.*
— LaMaster Family Prayer

GAME DAY 5

Chariots of Fire Faith

Who is Eric Liddell, and what does he have to do with faith?

Game Plan

Game Day Theme: Faith

God's Key Play: James 1:2–4, 12

Game Day Activity: Gardening

God's Key Play

*Consider it pure joy, my brothers and sisters, whenever
you face trials of many kinds, because you know
that the testing of your faith produces perseverance.
Let perseverance finish its work so that you may be*

*mature and complete, not lacking anything. Blessed
is the one who perseveres under trial because, having
stood the test, that person will receive the crown of life
that the Lord has promised to those who love him.*
— JAMES 1:2–4, 12

Scouting Report for Dads

Eric Liddell. Ever heard of him? If you are an Olympic historian or a 1980s movie buff, you likely know his story. You may also be familiar with the theme song from the movie, *Chariots of Fire*, or from *National Lampoon's Vacation* (think of the Griswolds running in slow motion to the entrance gate of Wally World). However, if you have not heard of him or the movie that made his story famous, my guess is that after reading the following few paragraphs, you will never forget him and what he taught you and me about complete faithfulness to Jesus Christ.

I was inspired to write this chapter after reading *7 Men and the Secret of Their Greatness*, written by Eric Metaxas. I saw the movie, *Chariots of Fire*, as a young man but didn't identify with Eric Liddell's faith walk and dedication to Jesus Christ until I read the pages of Metaxas' book. The following story of Eric Liddell is a brief summary of Metaxas' book chapter, simply titled, "Eric Liddell." I am grateful for Metaxas' compilation of Liddell's life, and my hope is that by sharing this story, you and your son will learn what true faith in God looks like.

Born in China in 1902 to Scottish parents who were missionaries, Eric Liddell was described as a "shy, quiet teenager who loved mathematics and science—especially chemistry—and sports."[1] As many missionary parents do, the Liddells enrolled Eric into a boarding school near London, England. It wasn't long before Eric's athletic talent showed itself. As a 12 year old, Eric earned first place in the high jump, long jump, and 100-yard dash. That was just the start. Eric would go on to win multiple events throughout his high school career.

When he entered college at the University of Edinburgh in his native Scotland, Eric signed up for sports only after his friend convinced him to do so. And as they say, the rest is history. Despite his wacky, windmill-like running style with high knees, he was being noticed not only at the university but by the public eye as well. Nicknamed "The Flying Scotsman," Eric shook the hands of each of his competitors, wished them well, and lent them his trowel to dig their starting blocks. Eric was not only a sensational sprinter but he was a gentleman and courteous competitor as well.[1]

With his ever-increasing fame, Eric was soon invited to speak about his faith at the Glasgow Students' Evangelistic Union. Eric was not a fan of public speaking; however, he received a letter from his sister that quoted Isaiah 41:10. Eric believed this letter was God speaking to him and using him to spread the word of God. Eric spoke to the group of 80 people in attendance about his faith and what God meant to him, "Of how he never questioned anything that happened either to himself or to others. He didn't need explanations from God. He simply believed in Him and accepted whatever came."[1]

Eric ran all the way to a spot on the Great Britain Olympic team for the 1924 Olympics in Paris! Here is where Eric's story of unwavering faith in God is exemplified. Eric found out that the trial heats for the 100-meter race were to take place on a Sunday. Eric made a simple decision; he would not race on Sunday, the Lord's Day. Despite multiple attempts by the British Olympic Committee to change Eric's mind, Eric did not waver in his decision. He would not race on a Sunday but would obey God.[1]

Instead, Eric prepared for the 400-meter and 200-meter races, which he also qualified for. On Sunday, July 6, 1924, while the other Olympians were racing for a spot in the 100-meter race, Eric attended a church service and went to a dedication at the Tomb of the Unknown Soldier. The following day, race day, Eric was cheering on his teammate, who took the gold medal, the first gold medal ever for Great Britain in this event. Eric went on to win the bronze medal in the 200-meter race and then prepared for the 400-meter race.[1]

Eric did qualify for the final heat of the 400-meter race but was not the favorite as his opponent had broken the world record in his qualifying heat. Eric also drew the outside lane, deemed the worst lane in the racing world because you can't see your opponents at the beginning of the race. With the odds stacked against him, Eric started the race as he did every other race—by shaking hands with his opponents and sharing his starting trowel.[1]

Eric was not running for himself—he was running to glorify God. He started out of the blocks at a blistering pace, which many thought he could never sustain. Well, he did, and he won the gold medal for the 400-meter race in world record time.

Despite all of his fame and potential future success as a sprinter, Eric hung up his racing spikes in lieu of a life committed to God. Eric eventually became a missionary in China as well as a pastor. He married and had three children. Eric's life was taken too soon, at the age of 43, by a brain tumor. He died in a Japanese war camp in China in 1943.[1]

We don't remember Eric Liddell for winning the gold medal in the 400-meter race of the 1924 Olympics; we will remember him for his faith in and dedication to God. Eric devoted his life to serving God and trusted in Him completely. Do you have this type of faith in God? If not, how can you teach your son to completely rely on God, serve God, and have faith in God?

If you or your son would like to read more about Eric Liddell's life, I highly recommend reading Eric Metaxas' book, *7 Men and the Secret of Their Greatness.* Metaxas' rendition of Eric Liddell's life and faith in God inspired me to not only write this chapter but to refocus my faith in Christ—for that, I will always be grateful.

Pre-Game Planning

As you prepare for today's Game Day, I want you to think of your own faith in Jesus Christ. I will get to the Game Day preparations in a bit (hint: think about where your gardening gloves are in your garage), but for now, I have a few stories about faith that are geared to get you thinking about your own faith.

Do you ever wonder if there are aliens in outer space? Weird question, I know! Did God create other intelligent beings on other planets? With movies like *Close Encounters of the Third Kind*, *Alien*, and *Contact*, I can honestly say that I have often considered it a possibility—more so as a young boy than an adult. Recently, my pastor, Dr. Paul Brushaber, shared a story from the *Wall Street Journal* that speaks to this very topic.

Pastor Paul read several excerpts from the article entitled "Science Increasingly Makes the Case for God."[2] Ironically, the December 25, 2014, article was written by none other than Eric Metaxas! All right, ready for some out of this world numbers? Here we go.

In 1966 astronomer Carl Sagan announced that there were two criteria for a planet to support life: the right kind of star and a planet at the right distance from the right kind of star. Metaxas goes on to state, "Given the roughly octillion—1 followed by 27 zeros—planets in the universe, there should have been about septillion—1 followed by 24 zeros—planets capable of supporting life."[2]

Believe it or not, the collective project, Search for Extraterrestrial Intelligence (SETI), formed in the 1960s, sent signals out into space specifically coded to locate other forms of intelligence. SETI is not science fiction; it was funded by Congress until 1993 and remains privately funded today. Well, as of 2015, "researchers have discovered bupkis—0 followed by nothing."[2]

So what happened to the potential 1,000,000,000,000,000,000,000,000 (septillion) planets with potential for intelligent life forms? God revealed more and more bits of science throughout the past half century. In fact, instead of only two parameters to support life, scientists have now found more than 200 parameters necessary for a planet to support life. Instead of one septillion planets that have the potential to support life, there is now zero possibility that other planets may support life.[2]

To further illustrate this point, A. Cressy Morrison shared "Seven Reasons Why a Scientist Should Believe in God." I would like to share reason number one with you now:

> *By unwavering mathematical law, we can prove that our universe*
> *was designed and executed by a great engineering intelligence.*[3]

Cressy Morrison goes on to add the following supporting facts:

- The earth rotates on its axis 1000 miles per hour at the equator. If it turned at 100 miles per hour, our days and nights would be ten times as long as they are now, and the sun would burn up our vegetation.
- Our sun has a temperature of 10,000 degrees Fahrenheit. Earth is precisely the correct distance from this great star that we neither freeze over nor burn up. Any slight difference in distance would greatly affect human life.
- Earth is tilted at precisely 23 degrees at its axis, thus giving us our seasons. Any slight variation in this angle would cause vapors from the ocean both north and south and would cause continents of ice.
- Our moon is also precisely distanced from Earth. If the moon were only 50,000 miles away, daily tides would submerge all continents and would eventually erode our highest mountain ranges.
- If the crust of the earth would be only 10 feet thicker, there would be no oxygen!
- Finally, if the ocean was only a few feet deeper, carbon dioxide and oxygen would be absorbed and not released into the air.[3]

I know this is a lot to take in and process, but this helps to strengthen my faith in our all-knowing and powerful God. If God designed the precise angles of the earth's axis and exact distances and depths to allow human life, I have faith that He can do all things—all things for my family and me.

List five things that affirm your faith in God. This will help prepare you for when your son asks you during Game Day!

1. _____
   _____
2. _____
   _____
3. _____
   _____
4. _____
   _____
5. _____
   _____

Now that you have searched your mind and soul for your faith in God, let's get ready for Game Day. Did you remember where you put your gardening gloves?

Pre-Game Day Prayer

Dear Heavenly Father,

_____ (Your son's name) and I have trouble understanding Your might and power. We believe that you created the heavens and the earth, but really cannot comprehend what that means. Dear God, help _____ (your son's name) and I continue to stretch our faith in You. Help us to live to glorify You, to fix our eyes on You, and to live our lives while putting You first. We ask for your guidance today as we explore and deepen our faith in You.

In Jesus' name we pray, Amen.

Playbook

Gardening is the theme for today's Game Day. The playbook calls for a review of the Parable of the Sower in Luke 8:4–15. Go ahead and read the parable, and I will summarize it below:

In the Parable of the Sower, God spoke of four types of people that hear His word through the imagery of seed and soil. For the purposes of today's Game Day, I have taken the liberty of literary license to label each type of seed using golfing terms.

Birdie Soil: Seed scattered along the path—trampled on and eaten by birds

Desert Course Soil: Seed scattered on rocky ground—withered with no moisture

Out of Bounds (O.B.) Soil: Seed scattered on thorns—choked out by the thorns

Putting Surface Soil: Seed scattered on good soil—yielding a crop 100 times its own

For today's game, you will need the following items:

1. FNL4FS book
2. Bible with James 1:2–4, 12 and Luke 8:4–15 bookmarked
3. Packet of mustard seeds. These are readily available where garden supplies are sold.
4. Four Styrofoam cups or plastic cups
5. One handful of the following:

    a.   Bird seed of any kind

    b.   Any type of rock (i.e., sand, gravel, or any type of landscaping rock)

    c.   Any type of pulled weed with root and dirt intact

    d.   Fertilized potting soil (i.e., Miracle-Gro or any similar off-brand)

6. Pitcher for watering seeds
7. Permanent markers to label and decorate the cups.

Well, that should do it for materials. Are you ready to get started? All right, after you have gathered all of your supplies, have your son follow the instructions below:

1. Do the following for each individual container:
   a. Label the first cup "Birdie," and fill it with birdseed.
   b. Label the second cup "Desert Course," and fill it with sand, gravel, or rocks.
   c. Label the third cup "O.B.," and fill it with weeds (remember to include the root and some dirt).
   d. Label the fourth cup "Putting Surface," and fill it with pre-mixed, fertilized potting soil.

      Feel free to be as creative as you want to be. Your son may want to draw, color, or simply write the name of the seed on the cup.

2. Read the Parable of the Sower (Luke 8:4–15) to your son, and ask him to explain what he thinks the lesson is trying to teach him.

3. Next, place about five mustard seeds in each cup.

4. Then use a pitcher of water to water each cup equally.

5. Next, ask your son what he thinks will happen to each of the seeds in the different cups. Have him write down his thoughts below:

Projections

Date: _____
Birdie Soil:

_____

Desert Course Soil:

_____

O.B. (Out of Bounds) Soil:

_____

Putting Surface Soil:

_____

6. Depending on your weather and climate, set your cups outside in direct sunlight. If this is not an option, place near a window that has the opportunity to get sunlight for most of the day. Your seeds should start sprouting within a couple of days.
7. When your seeds begin to sprout, have your son document what seeds sprouted, and have him compare the results with what he predicted a couple of days ago.

Final Results

Date: _____
Birdie Soil:

_____

Desert Course Soil:

_____

O.B. (Out of Bounds) Soil:

_____

Putting Surface Soil:

_____

8. Explain the lesson that Jesus teaches us in the Parable of the Sower to your son (summarized below):

The mustard seed symbolizes the Word of God.

The seeds that were spread in the "Birdie" soil symbolize the people that hear the Word of God, but then the devil comes to take the Word from their hearts and souls. These people are not saved.

The "Desert Course" soil symbolizes the people that initially receive the Word of God with open hearts. Unfortunately, the seed of God's Word does not take root; when life gets tough, they soon lose faith in God.

The seeds that fall in the "Out of Bounds" (O.B) soil represent the people that hear God's Word but are choked off by the things of this world—material things, anxiety, wealth, and worry. They in turn never fully realize the true meaning of God's Word.

Finally, the seeds that scattered in the "Putting Surface" soil symbolize the people that hear God's Word with open and pure hearts, live life the way God intended, and spread their faith in Jesus Christ to others.

If all went well, the only soil that produced healthy sprouts was the "Putting Surface" soil. If not, you may have some amazing rocks and weeds that can produce sprouts! Get ready to spend some time with your son in the Post-Game Day Analysis.

Post-Game Day Analysis

Now that you know about the Parable of the Sower, it's time to ask a few questions to see how this 2,000-year-old story relates to you and your son's lives today. So grab a hot dog or burger and order extra mustard—I prefer Grey Poupon—and ask each other the following Post-Game Day Analysis questions.

1. What type of soil do you feel represents your faith in God today—Birdie Soil, Desert Course Soil, O.B Soil, or Putting Surface Soil? Why?
2. Did you think that the mustard seeds would grow in all types of soil? Why or why not?
3. Have you ever felt like the "things of this world" have affected your relationship with God? If so, what things?
4. What is one thing that is still hard for you to believe about God?
5. Tell me about a time in your life when your faith in God gave you comfort and peace.

Post-Game Day Press Conference

Media Questions for Dad:

Have your son start recording and ask you the following questions:

1. Dad, do you have the type of faith that Eric Liddell, from *Chariots of Fire*, had? Can you explain?
2. Tell me about a time in your life when your faith in God gave you comfort and peace.
3. What was your favorite part about today's Game Day?
4. Dad, how have you seen my faith in Jesus Christ growing?

Media Questions for Son:

Start recording ` and ask your son the following questions:

1. _____ (Your son's name), what was one thing you learned about faith today? Explain.
2. Would you ever refuse to play in a tournament on Sunday like Eric Liddell did? Why or why not?

3. After hearing me tell you the story about all of the things required to have life on planet Earth, do you believe that God created any other forms of life on other planets?

4. As in the Parable of the Sower, do you know anyone that has "Birdie" Soil, "Desert Course" Soil, or "O.B." Soil? If so, how can we help them?

5. Finally, how would you rate today's Game Day? Circle the mustard sprouts below (1 mustard sprout = Not so good and 5 mustard sprouts = Awesome)

Game Day 5 is now in the books. As always, please share any videos or stories from your Game Day with our FNL4FS fans on the Friday Night Lights for Fathers and Sons Facebook page. We want to hear about your mustard seed stories and would love to see how creative you and your son were at decorating your cups!

Link's X's and O's

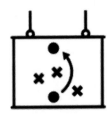

X: I learned that if you have faith the size of a mustard seed, then you can have faith in God. By the way, mustard seeds are really small.

O: I want to have complete faith in God!

Post-Game Day Prayer

Dear Heavenly Father,

Thank You for the intentional time that _____ (your son's name) and I have been able to spend together in Your word and Your parables during today's Game Day. We continue to be humbled by Your power and glory. We have learned that the testing of our faith produces perseverance and blessed is the one who perseveres under trial because, having stood the test, that person will receive the crown of life that You have promised (James 1:2–4, 12). _____ (Your son's name) and I have also learned that just because we have heard Your word does not mean that we are living out our faith as You have planned for us. We must be steadfast in our faith no matter what life throws at us. We pray that our faith sprouts like the mustard seeds planted in the nutrient-rich soil, allowing us to share our faith with others.

In Jesus' name we pray, Amen.

> *Have faith in God; God has faith in you.*
> — EDWIN LEWIS COLE

GAME DAY 6

Service Before Self

The United States Air Force core value all men should know

Game Plan

Game Day Theme: Service

God's Key Play: Matthew 20:28

Game Day Activity: Service Project

God's Key Play

*...just as the Son of Man did not come to be served, but
to serve, and to give his life as a ransom for many.*
— MATTHEW 20:28

Scouting Report for Dads

One core value that your son needs to learn from the United States Armed Forces, specifically the Air Force, is "Service Before Self."[1] Just as Jesus stated in Matthew 20:28, we were not brought into this world to be served but to serve many others. As you read the two stories below, think about the Service Before Self core value as well as Matthew 20:28.

Bullets pierced the city streets, seeking the young men in their urban warfare uniforms. One of the thousands of bullets fired found its way into one of the young men, directly into his upper thigh. Corporal Smith was bleeding bright red blood and needed medical intervention—now![2]

Corporal Jamie Smith served his country as an Army Ranger, following in the footsteps of his father. There was never a doubt that Jamie would become a Ranger despite his father's frequent lectures to dissuade him from the horrors of combat. He should know; he lost his leg while in combat in Vietnam.[2]

Smith's fellow soldiers soon realized the seriousness of their fellow comrade's injury and shouted for a medic. Delta Force veteran medic, Sergeant First Class Kurt Schmid, answered the call. He exposed Smith's leg wound and knew he had a bleeder. Schmid started two intravenous lines and immediately began infusing fluid as fast as possible.[2]

Schmid focused solely on serving his fellow soldier. He knew that most likely the bullet that had hit Smith had severed his femoral artery. He also knew that the only way to save Smith was to clamp the femoral artery and get him to an operating room. Schmid was a highly trained combat medic, most likely trained to the level of a physician's assistant or nurse practitioner. He had trained not only on the battlefield but also in a Level I trauma center to become efficient in his trade. He tried all of the tricks of his trade but eventually lost the battle of blood loss as Smith died.[2]

From the story you just read, you most likely don't remember the young men's names, but you may remember the story of this tragic event as being from either the book or movie of the same title, Mark Bowden's *Black Hawk Down*. Both Smith and Schmid are heroes in my book, not only for what they did on the battlefield but also for selflessly serving our country.

The Battle of Mogadishu occurred in 1993, the same year that a boy by the name of Joe Landolina was born. In 1993 Schmid's bag of tricks did not include what it would have today—combat action tourniquets, QuikClot, and thawed plasma.

No one at the time could have ever predicted that the then 10-month-old Joe Landolina would eventually develop a product that may well have allowed Schmid to save Smith's life only 17 years later. That's right; Joe Landolina invented Vita-Gel, a topical gel product that stops bleeding within 10 seconds of application. Joe Landolina was brought into this world to use his God-given gifts to serve others. Vita-Gel hits the veterinary market in 2015, and it is predicted that it will be approved for use in humans the following year. Landolina is now the CEO of his own company and has even added a TED Talk to his resume.[3]

If you think Joe Landolina is an anomaly, you are way off. Landolina is part of a wave of young people empowered to "Do Hard Things." Landolina is a rebelutionist—part of the rebelution sparked by 16-year-old twin brothers Alex and Brett Harris. The Rebelution, according to the Harris' website, is "a teenage rebellion against low expectations."[4] In their book entitled *Do Hard Things*, these highly motivated and inspirational Christian twin brothers challenge the expectations put on them by society.[5]

Alex and Brett explain that the word *teenager* has only been around since first being published in *Readers' Digest* in 1941. Since then, the Western culture has continued to lower the expectations of those aged 13 to 19, in turn lowering the expectations for younger children as well.[5]

According to their website, "rebelutionaries have raised hundreds of thousands of dollars for missions and charity, won prestigious film festivals, earned Grammy Award nominations, fought human trafficking around the world..."[4]

The Rebelution's mission statement is 1 Timothy 4:12: "Don't let anyone look down on you because you are young, but set an example for the believers in speech, in conduct, in love, in faith and in purity."[4]

Now, if that doesn't pump you up to show your son how to serve others and do amazing things, I don't know what will. It's time to get into your zone and find some way to become a Playoff Parent for today's Game Day. This one will require a little planning on the part of us padres but will be well worth it for you, your son, and for others. Believe me, with a little effort, you and your son will have the hottest ticket in town—tickets that cannot be scalped or purchased on StubHub! We were made not to be served but to serve others.

Pre-Game Planning

All right, dads, this is one of those Game Days in which the more you put into it, the more you will get out of it. Today's Game Day will involve a service project that you and your son plan together. I have provided you with several ideas to get your brains thinking in the right direction, but please know there are hundreds of different service and volunteer opportunities all around you.

Heavy Hitters

- Volunteer at your local Habitat for Humanity: habitat.org.
- Pack meals at the nearest Feed My Starving Children Mobile Pack: fmsc.org.

Concession Stand Service Projects

- Volunteer at your local soup kitchen or food shelf.
- Volunteer to make dinner for a local homeless shelter—make sure your son is involved with planning the menu, shopping, and cooking.
- Deliver meals to seniors that are shut in with Meals on Wheels: mealsonwheelsamerica.org.

Farm Team Volunteers

- Volunteer to help with the local county fair 4-H animal programs.
- Volunteer at your local animal shelter, offering to feed and play with the animals or doing other odd jobs that need to be done.

The Senior Tour

- Spend a few hours at a nearby nursing home. Arrange a bingo game, and bring treats that all can enjoy. Don't forget the most important thing—your smiles.
- Organize transportation for church members that cannot drive to church on their own. Most likely your church leadership has a list of members that need this assistance.

Olympics

- Volunteer at a Special Olympics game or event: SpecialOlympics.org.

Marathon Man

- Run, walk, or ride your bike in a charity-sponsored event, and have friends, family, and coworkers sponsor you and your son.
    - National Multiple Sclerosis Society: nationalmssociety.org
    - Leukemia & Lymphoma Society: lls.org/team-lls
    - ALS (Amyotrophic lateral sclerosis), aka Lou Gehrig's Disease: alsa.org

These are just a few ideas to get you thinking. If you already have a charity or program that you are involved with, great! If you need some more ideas, just google volunteer or service project ideas! Once you and your son have decided what service project you want to participate in, it's time to begin your Game Day preparations.

Pre-Game Day Prayer

Dear Heavenly Father,

You have shown us in so many ways that we are meant to serve others and not ourselves. But for so many reasons, we become so distracted and selfish, serving only ourselves. As _____ (your son's name) and I embark on today's Game Day service project, we seek Your guidance. Help us to understand why You sent Your one and only Son to serve, not to be served. We can get so caught up with ourselves that we easily forget what our true purpose is—to serve others. I ask that _____'s (your son's name) eyes are opened to the power of serving today. Help him to see that whatever his age, he can make a positive impact in the lives of other people. Help him to understand that he can "Do Hard Things" even though our culture continues to expect less and less of him. As we serve others today, we pray that our service becomes a beacon to the lives of those around us.

In Jesus' name we pray, Amen.

Playbook

You may have noticed that the Pre-Game Planning can take a bit of time, but believe me, it is all worth it! This Game Day is no different. The Playbook for today's Game Day will require the following materials:

1. FNL4FS book
2. Your Bible with Matthew 20:28 bookmarked and memorized
3. Make arrangements with the organization you plan on serving. Most likely you will need to make arrangements at least a week, if not more, in advance.
4. Have your son help with the arrangements and preparations for this service project.
5. Arrive at whatever event you choose ready to serve!

Post-Game Day Analysis

It's time to take a few minutes to analyze today's Game Day service project. Pick a spot at the location you served today or find a comfortable, quiet, and somewhat private place to answer the following Post-Game Day Analysis questions.

1. Describe how you are feeling right now.
2. How do you know that what we did today makes a difference?
3. Dad, in what ways do you serve others?
4. _____ (Your son's name), what is one thing about today that made an impression on your heart?
5. What are other ways that we can serve this group of people?

Post-Game Day Press Conference

Lights, camera, action! You know the drill—it's time to record your memories of today's Game Day with the media.

Media Questions for Son:

Start recording and ask your son the following questions:

1. What was your favorite part about today's Game Day?
2. If all of your friends were here right now, what would you tell them about your experience today?
3. We know that Matthew 20:28 tells us that Jesus came to serve and not to be served. How do you think that this verse and your experience today will change you as a person?
4. How would you rate today's Game Day? Circle the Runners below (1 runner = Not so good and 5 runners = Awesome)

Media Questions for Dad:

Have your son start recording and ask you the following questions:

1. Dad, what did I do well today?
2. What other types of service projects or volunteer projects have you done in your life?
3. Dad, do you think we made a difference today?
4. What is the one thing that you will remember most about today?

Link's X's and O's

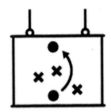

X: It feels good to help other people by serving.

O: I thought it was cool that Jesus came to serve, not to be served.

Post-Game Day Prayer

Dear Heavenly Father,

Today _____ (your son's name) and I were blessed with the opportunity to serve You and Your Kingdom. We were able to help make a difference in the lives of others today. No matter how small or large a part we played in serving others, we shared our time focused on others rather than ourselves—something that we know we don't do enough of. We often get lost in our own issues and become selfish. But today we learned that by serving others, we are fulfilling the purpose You have for us. We pray that our

experience today leads to further service and volunteer projects and helps us to focus more on others rather than ourselves.
In Jesus' name we pray, Amen.

United States Air Force core value: Service Before Self

GAME DAY 7

How to Recruit a Winning Team of Friends

Are the friends we choose really that important?

Game Plan

Game Day Theme: Developing Godly Friends

God's Key Play: Proverbs 12:26

Game Day Activity: Disc Golf

God's Key Play

The righteous choose their friends carefully,
but the way of the wicked leads them astray.
— PROVERBS 12:26

Scouting Report for Dads

Dads, be honest—how many close guy friends do you have? I don't mean the kind of friend that you play golf with during Tuesday night men's league. I don't mean the kind of friend that you talk college football or NBA basketball with. And I don't mean the kind of friend that you go to happy hour with and talk about work with. The kind of friend that I am talking about is the one that you can talk to about God with, the kind of friend that is there for you when you are going through tough times, and the kind of friend that makes you a better person just by being around him.

I'll admit it—it has only been within the past couple of years that I have truly had the kind of friend that I just described. I certainly have many other guy friends. My best friends from high school and I still keep in touch via phone and try to get together once per year for our annual backyard barbecue. We are geographically separated, but we are also separated spiritually. Is it actually possible for me, a Christian, to not know if either of my best friends from high school are believers or not? I have had numerous opportunities to talk with both of them about this topic but simply strike out each time I step up to the proverbial plate.

I don't think I am alone with this guy friendship struggle. Adult men have few close friends that they can talk to about their feelings, about God, about what they are afraid of, and especially about how to raise their son. In his book, *The Friendship Factor*, Alan Loy McGinnis states that most experts believe that only about 10% of adult males have any real friends. McGinnis goes on to state that close friendships don't just happen. Rather, close relationships result from the application of principles recorded throughout the Word of God.[1] God does not want us to be alone, but He cautions that we should choose our friends wisely. Proverbs 12:26 reminds us that "The righteous choose their friends carefully, but the way of the wicked leads them astray." In order for us to serve God's purpose in our lives, we must have Christian friends to help us accomplish our mission.

How about another survey? I know, these are challenging because they force you to dig deep into your personal life. While you may be hitting homeruns at work, you may be "riding the pine" with your male relationships. Just remember, your son is watching your every move, including your friendships. Whether or not you have strong male friendships will greatly impact whether or not he does as well. Here we go: Batter Up!

Male Friendship Survey

1. I have _____ male friend(s) that I consider my best friend(s)—meaning that I can talk to him/them about God, finances, family, work issues, life struggles, and success, anytime, anywhere.
    a. one
    b. two
    c. no
    d. three or more

2. The friend(s) that I hang out with have a _____ influence on my faith life, family life, and work life.
    a. neutral
    b. somewhat positive
    c. negative
    d. globally positive

3. The last time I did something with my friend(s), I felt _____.
    a. like I always do, comfortable
    b. somewhat inspired

    c.   guilty for spending too much time away from my family, for doing things that my family would not be proud of, or for hanging out with guys that don't have the same values as I do.

    d.   inspired and challenged to become a better overall person

4.   While growing up, I remember my dad spending time with _____ .

    a.   one or two friends that he played sports with or worked with

    b.   one friend that he looked up to, to become a better person at work, church, or parenting

    c.   only our family; I don't remember my dad having any male friends

    d.   several friends that my dad would look to for spiritual, parenting, financial, and work advice; a few of these friends went to our church

5.   I want to encourage my son to have male friends that_____ .

    a.   he can have fun with

    b.   he can entrust with personal struggles

    c.   he can do things with that he would choose not to do with his family

    d.   he can learn from, lean on, be inspired by, and grow closer to God with

All right, that wasn't too bad, was it? Here is how to score this short survey.

Count up all of the b's, a's, c's, and d's that you circled, and enter that number below:

    b _____ a _____ c_____ d_____

Be honest, dads! Sometimes the truth is tough to handle, but it gives us a starting point from where to improve. Next, circle the letter with the highest number. Whatever letter you circled above describes the type of friend role model you are for your son.

D. Playoff Friend
You are an excellent friend and role model for your son. Keep up the great work! Over time, you have intentionally chosen friends that inspire and challenge you to become a better person in many areas of your life. The types of friendships you have benefit you, your family, and your community.

B. Starting Lineup Friend
You have a couple of great friends that help you to improve who you are. You may want to challenge yourself to befriend someone that will inspire you to become better at something you feel you need improvement in.

A. 6th Man Friend
You are off to a great start, but the friends you have may just be guys to hang out with, nothing more and nothing less. I would challenge you to deepen these relationships by discussing topics such as family, parenting, finances, and religion.

C. Benchwarmer Friend
As you most likely already know, you may not have any male friends or choose to do things with other guys that make you feel guilty—like drinking too much, participating in activities that you would never want your son to participate in, or simply spending more time with these "friends" than you do with your own family.

This survey is not easy. I created it to challenge you to take a close look at who you truly are as a dad. Without scouting your own issues, how can you be an effective father to your son? As you continue to spend time with your son, you will see how important male friendships are in the transition from boy to young man—a man after God's own heart.

Remember to review your Male Friendship Survey results. Be honest, and take a few minutes to contemplate your answers. If you don't ask yourself the tough questions, your son most likely will!

So what are you waiting for? For this Game Day, you will need to challenge yourself and your son to invite male friends to Game Day with you!

Pre-Game Planning

I want to tell you a brief story of what a true male friendship looks like. The two friends come from entirely different backgrounds and upbringings. Jon comes from big money and power, while Dave comes from a small-time farming community. Jon is several years older than Dave but continues to be impressed by the work ethic and bravery of his young friend. In fact, Dave proves himself so much that he is eventually told that he will take over the company that Jon's dad owns.

For most of us, this would cause jealousy and bitterness, but Jon accepts this decision, mostly because he knows that his dad has become more and more corrupt and selfish in his business practices. He knows that Dave is a better leader than both he and his dad. Soon Dave ends up marrying Jon's sister, both now becoming brothers-in-law. Jon continues to mentor Dave in all aspects of the business despite the fact that not he but Dave will take over the company. Their friendship continues to grow stronger, even though jealousy, bitterness, resentment, and competition could easily have taken hold.

Jon and Dave share their life dreams together, stand up for each other in times of need, and celebrate successes together. Jon and Dave help each other's families as well when times are rough or when they need support on tough decisions.

As Jon's dad learns from his company's board of directors that Dave will be taking over his company, not his son, he begins to scheme to have Dave removed from the company permanently. Of course, Jon often hears of these plans and continually chooses his friendship with Dave rather than his relationship with his own dad. As you can imagine, when Jon's dad finds out that his son is essentially betraying him, he must now make a choice. Jon's loyalty to Dave is unbreakable. In the end, Jon and his father are killed in a tragic accident. Dave grieves for his best friend's death. Even after Jon dies, Dave makes sure that Jon's son is taken care of.

Do you have a male friendship in which you can show not only kindness and compassion but also courage and commitment like Jon and Dave did? If not, it may be difficult for your son to develop this kind of relationship as he grows older.

Do you know anyone with this kind of a male friendship? If not, I can show you one straight from the Bible. If you turn to 1 Samuel, you will find out that the story of Jon and Dave that you just read is a modern-day translation of the friendship between Jonathan and David—yes, the David who is known as "a man after God's own heart." The David who killed Goliath. The David who was chosen by God to rule His kingdom. The David who was the small shepherd boy whom no one besides God gave the time of day.

God meant for us to have close male friendships. God had Abraham, Jesus had Peter, and Paul had Timothy and Barnabas. Who do you have? Who will your son have?

In his article entitled "Why Can't Men Be Friends," Wesley Hill states, "What we need isn't disinterested, disembodied camaraderie, in which we keep distance from one another's hearts and stories. We need stronger bonds for brothers and sisters in Christ."[2]

Pre-Game Day Prayer

Dear Heavenly Father,

We know by reading Your Word that having male friendships is an important part of our lives. We thank You for not only the relationship with our sons, but also with _____ (your friend's name) and _____ (your friend's son's name). We ask that you continue to bless our male relationships as well as the relationships of our sons. _____ (Your friend's name) and I pray that You bring godly friends into our sons' lives. We pray that You help us to guide and support positive and supportive relationships in our sons' lives. We also pray that You continue to strengthen _____ (your friend's son's name) and _____'s (your son's name) relationship with You. We ask that by sharing Your Word and Your message with our sons tonight, all of us would better understand the importance of biblical male friendships in our lives. We thank You for this time together today and ask for Your protection throughout this Game Day activity.
In Jesus' name we pray, Amen.

Playbook

As I stated above, it does take some effort to engage with friends. For today's Game Day, you will need to invite a friend and his son to play disc golf with you and your son. For some of you, it will be challenging just to pick up the phone and ask someone to go hang out with you. Do not have your son make this call! This Game Day is as much about you and your friends as it is for your son's friends!

1. Materials you will need:
   a. One Frisbee or set of disc golf discs (fairway driver, mid-range, and putter). You can use a Frisbee you have at home or purchase a set at a sporting goods store or Target for as little as 20 bucks.
   b. Bible with Proverbs 12:26 bookmarked (Remember to memorize this verse!)
   c. FNL4FS book
   d. Smartphone or video camera
   e. A bottle of water for each disc golfer
   f. A pad of paper and pencil to use as a scorecard. There are a few free and inexpensive disc golf apps as well.

2. Location options:
   a. Local disc golf course. These are usually free, but some do require a small fee.
   b. If a disc golf course is not near you, you can easily create your own course using trees, fire hydrants, telephone poles, or other objects as your "hole."

3. Rules:
   a. For the first six holes, play match play disc golf. Count individual throws for each hole. At the end of six holes, see what the average of each golfer is.
   b. For the next six holes, have the dads challenge the sons in "father vs. son best toss disc golf." Just like in best ball golf, for each hole, use only the best dad toss versus the best son toss.
   c. Take a water break here, and let other disc golfers play through if it is busy. The take-home message for today's

Game Day is that we can usually have a better outcome when we work together. Sometimes we need the support of our close friends, but other times we need to support them as well.

d. For the last six holes, play "overall best toss disc golf." Use the best toss of all four of your players' throws. Then total up the overall best toss average and compare it to the match play and the father vs. son best toss score. Which one has more throws?

e. You will most likely have the least number of throws during the last six holes. Ask your sons why they think this is.

Audible Options

For those of you who do not play disc golf or would like other options, these will work just as well:

1. Golf course (nine holes will be sufficient): This can be a par-3 course or a standard golf course.
   - Same rules as disc golf
2. Free throw shooting contest
   - Shoot 10 free throws each, and keep individual scores. Who made the most out of 10 attempts?
   - Next, shoot another 10 free throws as a group. If one of you misses, then the next person has a chance to make it, and so on. How many did your team make out of 10 this way?
   - For the final round of 10 free throws, let your sons choose which type of game they would like to play.

Post-Game Day Analysis

Tally up the final scores, and see if you shot over par, under par, or par. You can certainly talk about some of the great throws, the amazing shots, and long putts. Find a bench to sit on or a tree to sit under as you analyze today's game with as much insight as Johnny Miller does after the Masters Tournament. It's time again for the Post-Game Day Analysis.

Post-Game Day Analysis Questions (These questions should be answered by all participants.)

1. Do you have a best friend?
2. What makes him your best friend?
3. Review the story of David and Jonathan (1 Samuel). Would you like to have a friendship like David and Jonathan?
4. Is it easy or hard for you to make friends? Why?
5. What would make it easier for you to make friends?
6. How do you think God can help in your friendships?

Get out your smartphone or video camera because it's now time for the Post-Game Day Presser! Remember to ask your friend and his son if it is all right to record the Post-Game Day Press Conference. Offer him a copy if you like.

Post-Game Day Press Conference

For this Press Conference, let's start with both dads at the mic! Have your son and his friend alternate recording and asking the questions. Plan on this presser taking a bit longer because there will be four people answering the questions.

Media Questions for the Dads:

Have your son start recording and ask you and your friend the following questions. Make sure that both you and your friend answer each question.

1. What was the final score on the last six holes?
2. How did you become friends?
3. How has your relationship grown over the years?
4. Have you ever gotten into an argument?
5. How do you define what a best friend is?
6. Have you ever had a friend that is no longer a friend? Why?

Media Questions for Your Sons:

Dads, alternate asking the questions and recording for your sons. Make sure that both your son and his friend answer all of the questions.

1. What was your favorite part about today's game?
2. How do you define what a best friend is?
3. What did you learn about the Bible and male friendships today?
4. How can you become a better friend?
5. How would you rate today's Game Day? Circle the Frisbee dudes below (1 Frisbee dude = Not so good and 5 Frisbee dudes = Awesome)

Link's X's and O's

X: A best friend is someone you can be yourself around.
O: It's fun to hang out with friends you can talk about God with!

Post-Game Day Prayer

Dear Heavenly Father,

We would all like to thank You for the wonderful friendships You have blessed us with. Please continue to strengthen our male friendships, our relationships with our sons, and, most important of all, our relationships with You. Thank You for the intentional time we have had together today. We ask again that You help _____ (your friend's name) and me to help guide _____ (your friend's son's name) and _____ (your son's name) to choose their friends wisely, not friends that will lead them to wickedness. We know that Your Word is our best resource for relationships. Help us to seek Your Word for not just friendships but for all matters of this world. In Jesus' name we pray, Amen.

It's time to put your discs away and get ready for the next Game Day! We will be exploring entitlement and contentment. Get ready to toss out the trophies and see what 1 Timothy has to teach us about these two topics.

> *You are the average of the five people*
> *you spend the most time with.*
> — JIM ROHN

GAME DAY 8

Take the Trophy Away from En"title"ment

You must beat entitlement with contentment.

Game Plan

Game Day Theme: Entitlement vs. Contentment

God's Key Play: 1 Timothy 6:6–7

Game Day Activity: New Car Lot

God's Key Play

*But godliness with contentment is great
gain. For we brought nothing into the world,
and we can take nothing out of it.*
— 1 TIMOTHY 6:6–7

Scouting Report for Dads

I was an excited but focused nervous. There were six seconds left in the game. One of my teammates had just made a shot to pull us within one point of winning the championship game in our bracket. No time-outs left—full court press was on—we needed a steal—now!

We were a somewhat misfit Boys' Club basketball team coached by a life-time bachelor and shop teacher who volunteered countless hours of time to improve the lives of hundreds of young boys through the game of basket-ball. He entered us into a few out-of-town tournaments that included the company-sponsored and well-supported traveling teams with brand new uniforms, including matching warm-up outfits (with tear-away pants) and team duffle bags. We wore used (extremely used) black and gold polyester uniforms with extremely short shorts! Some of the uniforms did not match because the Boys' Club didn't have all of the sizes. I remember some minor complaints about how scratchy the uniforms were, but overall, we didn't re-ally care about all of the new, matching stuff our competitors had. We just wanted to win our bracket in the tournament despite being one of the lowest seeds in our section.

The other team made a great pass to in-bound the basketball. The ball handler dribbled the ball a few times up the court but made may-be his only error of the game—he telegraphed his pass down court to a player about 10 feet from me. He lobbed the ball, hoping I didn't have enough hops to steal the pass....

There was nothing fancy about us, our uniforms, or our coach. What we did have was a passion for the game, a belief in our team, and a respect for our coach. Most important of all, we were content with what we had and who we were. Sure, we wouldn't have said no to the cool new uniforms or other luxuries our opponents had, but we were simply content.

I never really had any hops, and the fact is, I was not even blessed with quickness, but what I did have was the gift of anticipation. I read the defender's eyes, darted for the ball, and stole the ball at half court with four seconds left. With the help of the small crowd's countdown—4, 3, 2, 1—I knew I had to take the shot myself. As the ball left my hand, the blare of the buzzer sounded. My shot had banked off the backboard, and with that, I made my first and last buzzer-beater shot of my basketball career. We won the championship in our bracket! My teammates and I shook our opponents' hands and celebrated our win. We were awarded first place trophies, a trophy that stayed on my shelf for many years as a sign of what can be accomplished as a team, even if we were a team of misfits from the Boys' Club!

I share this story for several reasons. First, I wasn't even supposed to play in this game. I was a bench player, but our star player fouled out just a few minutes before the end of the game. Second, our team of misfits ended up having at least three starters on our high school team—one who went on to play college basketball and one college football (Division 1). Third, the players on our team were not show boaters. Our coach would not have allowed any one of us to throw our hands up in the air while running down the court, to beat our chest full of pride to show others how amazing we thought we were, or to taunt others when we blocked his shot or beat him on offense. Fourth, we *earned* our trophies! Unlike the culture of youth sports today, only the teams that placed first, second, and third received trophies. In fact, the trophies went from largest to smallest based on what place you earned. Teams that did not place did not receive "participation" trophies or blue ribbons or medals. Just because you showed up didn't mean you were entitled to a trophy.

We live in a culture where youth sports not only allows, but seemingly embraces the entitlement virus that has plagued professional athletics all the way down to the pee-wee leagues. Read the following quote, and answer the multiple choice question that follows it:

I knew my actions were wrong. But I convinced myself that normal rules didn't apply. I never thought about who I was hurting. Instead, I thought only about myself. I ran straight through the boundaries that a married couple should live by. I thought I could get away with whatever I wanted to. I felt that I had worked hard my entire life and deserved to enjoy all the temptations around me. I felt I was entitled. Thanks to money and fame, I didn't have far—didn't have to go far to find them.[1]

Can you name the person who made the above statement?

a. A-Rod (Alex Rodriguez)
b. Tom Brady
c. Kurt Busch
d. Tiger Woods
e. LeBron James

For those of you who answered d, Tiger Woods, you were correct. You see, Tiger believed he had worked so hard for his entire life (all 34 years of it!) that this entitled him to cheat on his wife and two young children. Unfortunately, sports in America is way beyond chest pounding and fist pumping—sports in America has an entitlement virus that many believe has reached epidemic levels.

In a 2010 article, "The Entitled Athlete," published just after Tiger's apology, Vinnie Rotondaro wrote:

Experts say that a sense of entitlement can begin playing a role in an athlete's life as early as Little League, Pop Warner football or AAU basketball. Once a child displays a special ability—shooting a ball, hitting a ball or throwing a ball—he or she is at risk of drawing attention that focuses solely on athletic ability at the expense of holistic wellbeing.[2]

The article goes on to quote Dan Doyle, the Executive Director for the Institute of International Sports and the author of *The Encyclopedia of Sports Parenting*: "Success at the youth league, high school, or intercollegiate level... can cause huge problems. It can lead to sundry exemptions: athletically gifted children may not have to run the same amount of laps, they may be excused for being late to practice, they may be passed along the academic ladder."[2]

It might not be surprising that this is happening in our country today. Christine Brennan, of *USA Today*, gives some insight on one of the possible sources of this entitlement epidemic:

> So even if we don't have more entitled athletes now than we did 15–20 years ago, it sure feels as if we do because we know so much more about them.
>
> Where there once were four TV channels, there now are 400. While a controversial evening out for an athlete even a decade or so ago would have been left to the imagination, and perhaps the police blotter, we now have a visual image to attach to the mess that athletes have gotten themselves into.

You might ask yourself, so what does all this have to do with my son? My son doesn't showboat. My son doesn't taunt other players. My son doesn't mimic his favorite NBA or NHL player. My answer to that is great! But I caution you that if he watches ESPN's *Sports Center* or clicks on SI.com to catch up on his favorite player's stats, he will be exposed to endless stories of entitlement.

If your son has received a participation trophy, ribbon, or medal just for showing up, he may believe he has failed if he does not receive one during the next sport he plays.

If your son plays on a traveling team and is the star pitcher, forward, or goalie, he may be receiving special treatment from not only other players, coaches, and parents but also, unconsciously, from you.

Enough with the entitlement entrails...let's learn how to combat entitlement with contentment. You guessed it; the Bible gives us clear direction on this topic as well!

Pre-Game Planning

To prepare for today's big game, I want you to think about your most prized possession. For some of you, this may come almost immediately. For others of you, this may take a few minutes. Once you have identified your most prized possession, answer the following questions:

Circle either Yes or No.

1.	Is your most prized possession something you earned?	Yes	No
2.	Is your most prized possession something you paid for?	Yes	No
3.	Is your most prized possession something you have on display?	Yes	No
4.	Is your most prized possession something that you bought on impulse?	Yes	No
5.	Is your most prized possession something that can be easily replaced?	Yes	No
6.	Is your most prized possession something that you expected to receive?	Yes	No
7.	Is your most prized possession something that someone gave you?	Yes	No

All right, now that your brain is in thinking mode, if you answered yes to any of the even-numbered questions, your most prized possession might be something you felt entitled to. If you answered yes to any of the odd-numbered questions, your most prized possession might be something you earned, something that was gifted to you, or something that was passed down to you.

The point of this questionnaire is not to make you feel guilty if your prized possession is something you bought for yourself as a reward for a job well done or a personal goal you met. The point of this questionnaire is to illustrate that possessions, even your most prized possessions, are still "things of this world."

As Paul clearly states in God's Key Play for today's game, "For we brought nothing into the world, and we can take nothing out of it." While your great-grandpa's leather football helmet or your favorite uncle's Honus Wagner baseball card might have some sentimental or monetary value, you can take none of it with you.

While being the speediest sprinter, the perfect putter, the greatest goalie, the smoothest shooter, or the most talked about tennis player might get you your 15 minutes of fame, God has other plans for you and your son.

So whether it be our prized possessions or temporary fame that we feel improves our self-worth, we have it all wrong in God's eyes. God wants us to be content with what we have because we have fully committed to Him and His ways. I am not saying that we should not have nice things or not strive to be great at what God has gifted us to be great at. I am saying that I believe God wants us to see Him first—before we worry about our net worth, our possessions, or our status. God tells us that He will always provide for us. Check out Matthew 6:26, and see what Jesus says:

> *Look at the birds of the air; they do not sow or reap or store away in barns, and yet your heavenly Father feeds them. Are you not much more valuable than they?*

As our sons grow to become young men, it is our responsibility to combat entitlement with contentment. Our sons do not deserve trophies for everything that they do. They will make mistakes just as we will continue to make mistakes. Our sons must understand this and not expect to be continually awarded and applauded for both their successes and failures. It is our responsibility as dads to both model and teach this important character trait. I can think of no better way to illustrate this than to read the words of the Apostle Paul while he was imprisoned:

> *I know what it is to be in need, and I know what it is to have plenty. I have learned the secret of being content in any and every situation, whether well fed or hungry, whether living in plenty or in want (Philippians 4:12).*

Pre-Game Day Prayer

Dear Heavenly Father,

You are an amazing God! We are humbled before Your presence. As _____ (your son's name) and I spend time together today, help us to understand what it means to be content in this life. Help us to combat our culture's sense of entitlement by learning the secret to contentment. We were born with nothing, and we will leave with nothing. Help us to discover that we must learn to earn the luxuries of this life and that we do not deserve them. As we spend time together today as father and son, please help the words Paul wrote over 2,000 years ago permeate today's Game Day by helping us to learn how to be content in any situation.
In Jesus' name we pray, Amen.

Playbook

I must admit, my prized possession is my Cornhusker Red, 1997 V-6, 4.0-liter Jeep Wrangler. And yes, I answered yes to the even numbered questions in the questionnaire we went through earlier. And yes, I felt that I was entitled to owning a Jeep Wrangler. Before I purchased my Jeep, I had been driving a 14-year-old four-door Saturn that Jen and I had acquired on a 60-month payment plan. The Saturn was actually still running well as we had been using it as our in-town car for several years, and it only had about 120,000 miles. But something inside of me thought I deserved a Jeep Wrangler. I felt I was entitled to it. I had earned it. I have now had my Jeep for about six months and do enjoy driving it, especially in the summer! However, I can't help but think of what it would have been like to still have my old Saturn and the $10,000 still in the bank. Both the Saturn and the Jeep got me back and forth from work just the same.

In honor of my entitled Jeep Wrangler purchase, today's game on entitlement versus contentment will take place not on the asphalt of a public park's basketball court but on the asphalt of a new and used car lot. So take a few minutes to select your favorite local new and used car lot for today's Game Day location.

1. Materials you will need:

    a. FNL4FS book
    b. Smartphone or video camera
    c. Bible with 1 Timothy 6:6–7 bookmarked

2. Location options:

    a. Your preferred new and used car dealership. For many of you, the car dealership may sell both new and used cars; however, make sure you take a few minutes to find out what your son's favorite vehicle is before you choose the dealership.
    b. Sporting goods store and a used sports store like Play It Again Sports or a garage sale.

3. Rules:

    a. Ask your son, "If you could have your favorite vehicle, what would it be and why?"

b.   Your Game Day activity will be to test drive vehicles, starting with your son's favorite vehicle (within reason). If your son says a Lamborghini Aventador, you may need to ask him for his second favorite car!

c.   Once you know his favorite car, locate the nearest new car dealership that sells his favorite vehicle. Make sure you test-drive the latest model of his favorite vehicle to ensure that it still has that new car smell! Notice and write down the sticker price.

d.   You may need to make special arrangements with the salesperson depending on what type of vehicle your son chooses. For example, my son's dream vehicle is a red Stingray Corvette.

e.   Take the new vehicle out for a test drive, making sure to have your son check out all of the bells and whistles, including the new car smell.

f.   Once you have completed the test drive, drive through a local used car lot. Dads, here is where you get to pick out a vehicle—but there's a catch. You get to pick out the next car you drive—the most beat up, oldest, dirtiest, ugliest, and cheapest vehicle on the lot! Once you have picked out this car, take it for a test drive spin!

g.   As you are driving the used car, have your son jot down a few things about this vehicle as well.

Dream Car vs. Used Car Inventory Sheet

Have your son fill out the following inventory sheet while you are test-driving cars today.

	Dream Car	Used Car
Make and Model		
Year		
Sticker Price		
Miles		
New Car Smell?		
CD Player?		
Smartphone Jack?		
Estimated Miles per Gallon		
Speed in Town		
Speed on Highway/ Interstate		
Miscellaneous Notes:		

h. After you have driven both vehicles and have completed the inventory sheet, ask your son, "What is the true purpose of a vehicle?" As we know, the true purpose of a vehicle is to transport ourselves from one place to another much faster than by walking. A car's fundamental purpose is transportation of people or supplies from one destination to another.

i. Next, ask your son if his dream car would get him from point A to point B more efficiently than the used car that you test drove. Be prepared to discuss this topic, but don't forget to make the point that a used car that is properly maintained serves the same purpose as a brand new car. The main difference is how advertising and the Western culture make us feel in a new car versus an old, rusty, dirty car.

<u>Audible Options</u>

For those of you who do not live near a new or used car dealership or who would rather have other options, here is your audible:

- As mentioned previously, you can shop for sporting goods like brand new baseball bats, new football gear, or new hockey skates at a sporting goods store. As your comparison, shop for the same equipment at a used sporting goods store or garage sale. Then compare the differences in the same manner as with the new versus used car example.

We live in a time and culture in which we have more material things, more advanced technologies, and more access to information than any other generation before us. But for many of us, this just isn't enough. Many of us believe that we deserve a better car, a bigger house, or the latest and greatest smartphone. If we go through a rough time in our lives, we feel that we have paid our dues and that we deserve a better future. Here's the head fake: That's not how it works according to the Bible.

Post-Game Day Analysis

Once you have test driven both vehicles and your son has filled out the inventory sheet, find a spot to grab a soda or some ice cream and spend some time discussing your experience.

Post-Game Day Analysis Questions

1. What was your favorite part of test-driving your (your son's) dream vehicle?
2. Was riding in your dream car better than what you expected? Why or why not?

3. What is one thing that you have felt entitled to?
4. As you review your inventory sheet, what stands out the most to you? Why?
5. Could both of the vehicles go at least 85 miles per hour (theoretically)? (This is the top speed you can legally drive in the United States—but only on a toll road in Texas.)
6. Why does this matter? Think entitlement versus contentment.
7. When do you feel most content?

Post-Game Day Presser! You know the drill.

Post-Game Day Press Conference

<u>Media Questions for Dad:</u>

Have your son start recording and ask you the following questions:

1. Dad, what was your dream vehicle when you were my age? Why?
2. What do you or have you felt entitled to?
3. Dad, have you learned the secret of contentment that Paul talks about in 1 Timothy?
4. What do you do when you really want or expect something and then don't get it?

<u>Media Questions for Son:</u>

Start filming, and ask your son the following questions:

1. In your own words, tell me the difference between entitlement and contentment.
2. Were you embarrassed to ride in the used car? If so, why? If not, why?
3. What do you think Paul's secret to contentment is?
4. How would you rate this Game Day? Circle the honks below (1 honk = Not so good and 5 honks = Awesome)

I hope you had a great experience test-driving your son's favorite vehicle. Don't feel like you are now entitled to go buy one next week! If you and your son had a memorable experience, please share your experiences on the Friday Night Lights for Fathers and Sons Facebook page! Let's keep the father and son Game Days going!

Link's X's and O's

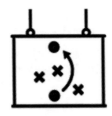

X: I want to work on how to be more happy with what I have.
O: Corvettes are awesome!

Post-Game Day Prayer

Dear Heavenly Father,

_____ (Your son's name) and I had a wonderful time test-driving vehicles today. We were able to learn that we don't need things like trophies and brand new vehicles to be content in this life. Even though they are really cool, we know that things don't bring us contentment. Only a relationship with You can bring us authentic contentment. We pray that You continue to guide us to being content in any situation and to learn how deflect the devil's stronghold on our sense of entitlement. We thank You for our time together, and we look forward to growing in our walk with You.
In Jesus' name we pray, Amen.

What separates privilege from entitlement is gratitude.
— BRENE BROWN

GAME DAY 9

Breaking Down the Play Calls:
P 31 and 1 C 16

The closest the Bible comes to describing womanhood and manhood

Game Plan

Game Day Theme: Biblical Definitions of Womanhood and Manhood

God's Key Plays: Proverbs 31:10–11 and 1 Corinthians 16:13–14

Game Day Activity: Dinner with Mom

God's Key Plays

*A wife of noble character who can find? She is
worth far more than rubies. Her husband has full
confidence in her and lacks nothing of value.*
— PROVERBS 31:10–11

> *Be on the alert, stand firm in the*
> *faith, act like men, be strong.*
> — 1 CORINTHIANS 16:13–14 (NASB)

Scouting Report for Dads

Biblical Womanhood

Her hair was a pure white, like the snow on an early winter's morning. Her eyes seemed to twinkle every time she smiled. She was kind, gentle, and optimistic. She was the type of person who made you feel like you were the only one in the room when you were talking to her. She always saw the bright side of things and was confident that things would work out well. She was my grandma.

I can remember when I was studying for a finals test and was extremely nervous about it. When I talked to her about it, she reassured me that I would do well and that it wasn't worth worrying so much about. She believed that worrying was truly a waste of time. I have always remembered this about my grandma and am reminded of the Bible verse from Matthew 6:25:

> *That is why I tell you not to worry about everyday life—whether you*
> *have enough food and drink, or enough clothes to wear. Isn't life more*
> *than food, and your body more than clothing?*

My grandma lived a full life, dying just before her 99th birthday. During her nearly 99 years, she certainly had much to worry about; however, she also had much to be thankful for. She chose to have a positive attitude, and I believe it had a great deal to do with her faith in God. She was a Proverbs 31 woman!

Born on a farm near Waterbury, Nebraska, in 1906, my grandma was raised on a homestead in South Dakota. I can remember my grandma talking of the winters on the Great Plains, of trading goods with the Native Americans of the area, and stories of her sisters and brother during her childhood.

My grandma and her sisters were musical prodigies and played in an all-girls orchestra that performed for college dances as well as throughout the Midwest. She attended college at Eastern State Teachers' College in 1932 and was a teacher for two years in a South Dakota country school. A career woman in the 1930s!

During the Great Depression, my grandma married and was blessed with a son. Unfortunately, her first marriage ended in divorce, not something so common during those times, especially for a Catholic woman. Despite her ex-husband's infidelity, she was determined to raise her young son. Not one to feel sorry for herself, my grandma went back to cosmetology school and earned her cosmetology license to work as a hair stylist/beautician. She eventually went on to open her own beauty shop. Then, in 1947, my grandma met my grandpa. Their marriage resulted in two daughters—and the rest is history!

My grandma was a loving mother to her three children, working both at home and outside of the home. She was also active in her community, volunteering for the Marine Corps League Auxiliary for 31 years! She was college educated and had entrepreneurial instincts. She experienced many advances in technology—the automobile, airplane, television, computers, air conditioning, and refrigeration!

At the age of 75, she was involved in a serious car accident, breaking her neck. Thanks to the amazing skill of the emergency medical technicians who transported her as well as the entire medical team that cared for her, she was granted nearly 24 more years of life. These 24 years were most influential to my siblings and me!

She was able to travel the world, see the birth of great-grandchildren, and impact generations after her. I tell you about my grandma because I believe she lived out the definition of biblical womanhood best described in Proverbs 31.

Take a moment to read Proverbs 31 and see if you agree. As you are reading this verse, also identify the Proverbs 31 women in your life.

Proverbs 31:10 states that the value of a virtuous wife is worth far more than rubies. What does that mean? I know what you are thinking—diamonds are supposed to be a woman's best friend, right? I thought you might ask, so check this out.

In 2012 a 32-carat Burmese ruby, the "Hope Ruby," was sold for more than $6.7 million![1] Another idea to illustrate how rare rubies are is from AOL in 2014: "The ruby is 50 times more rare than the diamond, and there has been no significant raw gemstone discovery in the last 20 years."[2]

I would say that rubies are rare as well as expensive, and now I have a better understanding of what the author of Proverbs 31 meant. What's even more intriguing is that Proverbs 31 is written from a woman's perspective. That's right, Proverbs 31 was written by King Lemuel, but it is clearly stated that the advice comes from his mother.

Proverbs 31 can be a bit overwhelming to interpret and understand. Therefore, I thought I would enlist the assistance of Melissa Ringstaff from avirtuouswoman.org. Ringstaff lists the 10 Virtues of a Proverbs 31 woman below:

1. Faith – A Virtuous Woman serves God with all of her heart, mind, and soul. She seeks His will for her life and follows His ways. (Proverbs 31: 26, Proverbs 31:29–31)

2. Marriage – A Virtuous Woman respects her husband. She does him good all the days of her life. She is trustworthy and a help mate. (Proverbs 31:11–12, Proverbs 31: 23, Proverbs 31: 28)

3. Mothering – A Virtuous Woman teaches her children the ways of her Father in heaven. She nurtures her children with the love of Christ, disciplines them with care and wisdom, and trains them in the way they should go. (Proverbs 31:28, Proverbs 31:26)

4. Health – A Virtuous Woman cares for her body. She prepares healthy food for her family. (Proverbs 31:14–15, Proverbs 31:17)

5. Service – A Virtuous Woman serves her husband, her family, her friends, and her neighbors with a gentle and loving spirit. She is charitable. (Proverbs 31:12, Proverbs 31:15, Proverbs 31:20)

6. Finances – A Virtuous Woman seeks her husband's approval before making purchases and spends money wisely. She is careful to purchase quality items that her family needs. (Proverbs 31:14, Proverbs 31:16, Proverbs 31:18)

7. Industry – A Virtuous Woman works willingly with her hands. She sings praises to God and does not grumble while completing her tasks. (Proverbs 31:13, Proverbs 31:16, Proverbs 31:24, Proverbs 31:31)

8. Homemaking – A Virtuous Woman is a homemaker. She creates an inviting atmosphere of warmth and love for her family and guests. She uses hospitality to minister to those around her. (Proverbs 31:15, Proverbs 31:20–22, Proverbs 31:27)

9. Time – A Virtuous Woman uses her time wisely. She works diligently to complete her daily tasks. She does not spend time dwelling on those things that do not please the Lord. (Proverbs 31:13, Proverbs 31:19, Proverbs 31:27)

10. Beauty – A Virtuous Woman is a woman of worth and beauty. She has the inner beauty that only comes from Christ. She uses her creativity and sense of style to create beauty in her life and the lives of her loved ones. (Proverbs 31:10, Proverbs 31:21–22, Proverbs 31:24–25)[3]

As I read through these ten topics, I cannot find one thing that my grandma did not exemplify during her life.

Are there any Proverbs 31 women in your life? Are you praying for your son's future spouse to be a Proverbs 31 woman? For today's Game Day, you will be showing your son how to invite his mom out to dinner. You will be teaching your son how to invite, plan, and act during a night out with a Proverbs 31 woman. More on that later, but first, you also need to teach him what it means to be a biblical man.

Biblical Manhood

Throughout this season, you have been working hard with your son to teach him what it means to be a man of the Bible, but we have not yet defined *Biblical Manhood*. Before we get too far, can you, in your own words, define or recite how the Bible defines manhood?

If you are able to, I congratulate you, and I applaud your father, pastor, or mentor. Most Christian men are unable to define what the Bible says about how men should act and behave and what their purpose truly is. I know that I certainly was not able to define biblical manhood until only a couple of years ago.

As I mentioned in the introduction of this book, I never really thought of what Biblical Manhood was until I took Robert Lewis' Authentic Manhood: Winning at Home and at Work course at my church. I became hungry for more knowledge of what the Bible had to say about men, our work, and our parenting responsibilities. This hunger led me to take the next class in

Lewis' *Authentic Manhood* series, The Great Adventure. Soon I was reading more, learning more, and applying more of what the Bible was teaching me about being a man. Next, I took a six-week class from the next generation of Authentic Manhood, a class named, 33 The Series: A Man and His Design. It was here that I learned the true definition of Authentic Manhood.

Imagine telling your son the following definition of what it means to be a real man according to the Bible:

> A real man is one who rejects passivity, accepts responsibility, leads courageously, and invests eternally.[4]

By the way, you should not only live this definition but you should memorize it and teach it to your son. This one is worthy of writing on the bathroom mirror with a dry-erase marker. Just a thought.

I highly recommend the *Authentic Manhood* series to you if you want to dig even deeper into your purpose as a man of God! See the Fatherhood Personnel Files at the back of this book for more of Lewis' resources.

All right, this is a great definition, but if you are like me, you may want the evidence from the Bible that helped Lewis develop this definition. Lewis does an amazing job of summarizing the evidence he uses to define Authentic Manhood. Follow along below as you will see the Bible verses pop out like you have never seen them before.[4]

A real man rejects passivity:

> Jesus, who though he was in the form of God, did not count equality with God a thing to be grasped, but made himself nothing, taking the form of a servant, being born in the likeness of men. And being found in human form, he humbled himself by becoming obedient to the point of death, even death on the cross. (Philippians 2:5–8, ESV)

A real man accepts responsibility (three parts):

- Jesus accepted responsibility for a will to OBEY.
  - John 4:34
- Jesus accepted responsibility for a work to DO.
  - John 17:4
- Jesus accepted responsibility for a woman to LOVE.
  - Ephesians 5:25

A real man leads courageously:

- Jesus led by providing directions for others, by providing protection for others, and by providing life for others.
  - Matthew 4:19, John 10:11, and 1 Corinthians 15:45

A real man invests eternally:

- Jesus invested in the eternal by living it and by teaching it.
  - Matthew 6:19–20 (ESV) states, "Do not lay up for your-selves treasures on earth, where moth and rust destroy and where thieves break in and steal, but lay up for yourselves treasures in heaven, where neither moth nor rust destroys and where thieves do not break in and steal."

Whew! Men, we have a lot of responsibility according to the Bible. As Jesus as our guide and with the Bible as our playbook, we can and will become the fathers that God created us to be. More importantly, we will be better equipped to father our own sons into becoming biblical men. I don't know about you, but having this definition of biblical, authentic manhood continues to inspire me to become better at everything I do, all for the glory of God!

Do your thoughts and actions meet the definition of biblical manhood? If not, in what area do you need to improve? I challenge you to identify one of the four topics to focus on during today's Game Day and beyond. Remember, whatever area you improve in will also positively affect your son as well!

We now have the Bible's definitions of both womanhood and manhood. As we move on to the Pre-Game Planning session, you may need to refer back to this Scouting Report as a reference. Now let's go to the coach's office to plan for today's Game Day.

Pre-Game Planning

As any good coach would know, before you plan, you have to know what your desired outcome is. I have alluded to the plan for today's Game Day, but now it's time for the details. Today's Game Day will involve teaching our sons how to properly treat a Proverbs 31 woman. I know that not all of us may have known what a Proverbs 31 woman was when we asked our brides for their hand in marriage, but now that we know, I will assume that your spouse is either already a Proverbs 31 woman or is a Proverbs 31 woman in progress!

You will need to enlist the help of your son in today's Pre-Game Planning session as he will ultimately be quarterbacking the play calls for this Game Day.

As a young boy growing up, I had no idea that I could or should be praying for a future spouse, a future Proverbs 31 woman. Even less than that, I truly did not know how to ask a girl on a date, what to do on the date, and how to treat her on the date. No offense, Dad, but I don't really remember talking to you much about the whole dating thing when I was a kid. What I did learn from my dad, though, was to imitate his behavior around my mom and sisters.

My dad always treated my mom like she was the most important, most beautiful, and most intelligent woman in the world—and still does today. He always spoke to my mom and sisters with respect and without raising his voice. When necessary, he did use the "dad" tone to get his message across. My dad modeled authentic manhood to me and has throughout my whole life. I would like to not only model authentic manhood to my son but also to teach him what authentic manhood is according to the Bible. If he has a strong foundation of what authentic manhood is, he will be better able to treat women respectfully, especially his future Proverbs 31 wife!

I feel there is no better way to teach this than to invite Mom out to dinner at a local restaurant. If, for whatever reason, Mom is not available, your son can certainly invite Grandma, an aunt, an older sister, or a female family friend. Let's get planning.

1. Review the biblical definitions of both womanhood and manhood with your son, and make sure he can summarize the definitions before you move on.
2. Inform your son that he will be inviting his mother out to dinner. Your son will need to research the following information:
    a. What is her favorite restaurant?
    b. What date and time will work best for her?
    c. Have him discuss with you (not mom) how much to budget for dinner.
    d. What is her favorite type of flower?
3. Once your son has fully researched the above questions, plan a budget with your son. Inform him that for today's Game Day, you (Dad) will be paying for dinner. Remember to include the cost of dinner, dessert, babysitter for siblings (if necessary), favorite flower, parking, and don't forget the tip!
4. Teach your son how to formally ask your wife out to dinner. Don't make this a "Hey, Mom, Dad said that I need to ask you to go to dinner with us" informal type of question.
5. Have your son look up the restaurant's phone number and reservation policy. He will be making the phone call. If your son is anything like my son, you will need to rehearse this with him a couple of times before he calls.

6. Remind your son to open the car door for his mom, to hold the door at the restaurant for her, and to pull out her chair for her at the restaurant. If you want to go the extra mile, teach him to stand every time his mom stands up as well.

7. Review table manners if necessary as well as stemware etiquette. If you need a review or a teaching aide, just google "Table Manners" or "Dining Etiquette."

8. Inform your son that he will be writing and giving a toast at the beginning of the meal.

9. Also inform your son that he will be leading the dinner party in prayer. I would recommend that he prepare this beforehand unless your son is great at "winging it."

10. Pre-plan a location for the Post-Game Day Press Conference. This may be at your dinner table, in the restaurant lobby, or at a location of your choice.

11. As you can see, chivalry is not dead! I want you to teach your son how a Proverbs 31 woman deserves to be treated. This is not old-fashioned stuff we are teaching him. If this is not something you currently do for your wife, start doing it now!

Pre-Game Day Prayer

Dear Heavenly Father,

During today's Game Day, we have already learned that Your word provides us with biblical definitions for womanhood and manhood. You sent Your son Jesus to give us a human example in addition to the written examples in the Bible. As _____ (your son's name) and I prepare for today's Game Day, continue to remind us how real men treat Proverbs 31 women. Help us to not only know the definitions but to also model the definitions of how real men behave. Father, I know that _____ (your son's name) looks to me to learn how to treat women. If there is something I need to improve or remove from my actions or behavior, please make me aware of this so I can more positively model my actions and behavior for my son. We ask that You help guide us as we plan our Game Day together to prepare for a memorable outing with our Proverbs 31 woman. I would also like to pray that you are developing a Proverbs 31 woman just for _____ (your son's name) as we speak and that someday they will meet and continue to glorify You! In Jesus' name we pray, Amen.

Playbook

The time has come. The Pre-Game Planning has prepared you and your son for a wonderful dinner with your Proverbs 31 woman. It is time to make a full-court press for today's Game Day Playbook. Remember, your son should be quarterbacking this series!

1. Invite Mom to dinner with you and Dad.
2. Request that Mom reads the Scouting Report for today's Game Day at least a day in advance.
3. Make reservations at Mom's favorite restaurant.
4. Plan the budget with Dad.
5. Arrange for a babysitter with Dad (if necessary)—Dad should make this call.
6. Prepare a toast.
7. Write a prayer for the meal.
8. Review table manners and door opening procedures.
9. Hit the shower, and dress up in proper Game Day attire—not necessarily a tie but not a tie-dye shirt. Go with at least a collared shirt and khakis.
10. Play Ball!

Materials you will need:
1. FNLF4FS Book

2. Bible
3. Smartphone or video camera
4. Notes for toast and prayer
5. Money as budgeted

Dinner conversation topics:

1. Begin with your toast.
2. Review the Game Day Scouting Report
   a. Proverbs 31 Woman
   b. Authentic Manhood definition
   c. Biblical references to both
3. Ask your mom and dad how they met.
4. Ask your mom and dad how they knew they were the right person to marry.
5. Ask your mom and dad if they have ever prayed for your future wife.
6. Ask your mom and dad if their parents taught them the biblical definitions of manhood and womanhood.
7. Ask your mom if she likes her meal.
8. Let your mom choose dessert today.
9. Treat the server with respect and gratitude, even if something is wrong with your order.
10. If the setting is right, as your dessert is served, begin your Post-Game Day Analysis questions.
11. Finally, when you all agree that you are done with your meal and have answered the Post-Game Day Analysis questions, respectfully ask for your bill. Work with your dad to pay the bill. Remember to tip appropriately.

Post-Game Day Analysis

I recommend that you ask the following questions at your dinner table during dessert. This will allow you to have time for nice dinner conversation but will also help guide you as to when to proceed with the Game Day. You may need to inform your server that you may be a few extra minutes. Do not be afraid to let them know why.

Questions for Son to Ask Mom and Dad Individually

1. What was your favorite part about tonight?
2. What are some things that you learned about biblical manhood and womanhood tonight?
3. In what areas do I show that I am learning to become a real man of God?
4. What areas do I need to learn more about to become a real man of God?
5. Tell your parents how much you love them!

Questions for Parents to Ask Son

1. How did you feel inviting, planning, and preparing for today's Game Day?
2. What can we do to improve how we parent you? Is there anything that you need from us that we are not giving you?
3. Tell your son that you are proud of him and that you love him!

Reminder: If you have not already paid your bill, now might be a good time because it is time for the Post-Game Day Press Conference. Let your mom know what this is and that she will soon be on camera answering a few questions from the media. Decide if you would like to do the Press Conference at your table, in the lobby, or at a pre-designated location you planned for. The media has entered the building. Are you ready for the Press Conference?

Post-Game Press Conference

<u>Media Questions for Dad:</u>

We will have your dad go first to give your mom an idea of what the Press Conference is like. Start recording and ask your dad the following questions:

1. Dad, what is the most important thing you learned about authentic manhood according to the Bible tonight?
2. Dad, can you describe in what ways that Mom is more valuable than rubies?
3. Name one way that you can improve your walk in authentic manhood?
4. Do you think I have what it takes to become a man like we talked about? Why?
5. Thank your dad for all of his help in planning today's Game Day and tell him that you love him again!

<u>Media Questions for Mom:</u>

Start recording, and ask your mom the following questions:

1. Mom, what one thing did you learn about a Proverbs 31 woman that you did not know before today's Game Day?
2. Mom, can you describe in what ways Dad lives out the biblical definition of manhood?
3. Name one way that you can improve on becoming more of a Proverbs 31 woman.
4. Tell your mom you love her again—and mean it.

<u>Media Questions for Son:</u>

Hand the camera to your dad. It's your turn to answer the tough questions from the media. Dads, start filming, and ask your son the following questions:

1. What was your favorite part about today's Game Day?
2. What is the one thing you learned today that you will always remember? Explain.
3. What is the one thing you learned about the Proverbs 31 woman that you did not know before today?
4. In what way is your mom a Proverbs 31 woman?
5. In what way do I act like the definition of a biblical man?
6. Name one way that you can improve to become more of a man of God.
7. How would you rate today's Game Day? Circle the rubies below (1 ruby = Not so good and 5 rubies = Awesome)

I hope you had a wonderful time during today's Game Day! I know that not only did I grow closer to my son, Lincoln, but I also grew closer to my wife as a result of our dinner conversation and Press Conference. I realized that I need to work more on leading courageously in my life as well as investing more eternally.

Please share any of your Game Day stories or Press Conference clips with the rest of us by posting them on the Friday Night Lights for Fathers and Sons Facebook page! I would love to hear how God is working in your relationships.

Link's X's and O's

X: My mom is a Proverbs 31 woman! I want to marry a Proverbs 31 woman!
O: I want to become the type of man God wants me to be.

Believe it or not, our next Game Day is the final game of the season. Before we move on to our season finale, let's pray.

Post-Game Day Prayer

Dear Heavenly Father,

We thank You for the precious, intentional time that we all had together during today's Game Day, learning about the kind of men and women you designed us to be. _____ (Your son's name) and I are so blessed to have _____ (Mom's name) in our life, providing Proverbs 31 blessings upon both of us. We pray that by better understanding Your Word and the life of Your Son, we continue to become more like the men You created us to be. As _____ (your son's name) continues to grow into a young man, may _____ (Mom's name) and I be guided by the Holy Spirit to bring him closer and closer to You. May he realize that he is never alone because You live in him. In Jesus' name we pray, Amen.

> *The most important thing a father can do*
> *for his children is to love their mother.*
> *—Henry Ward Beecher*

GAME DAY 10

Gear Up in the Armor of God

Championship Game

Game Plan

Game Day Theme: Championship Game

God's Key Play: Ephesians 6:11

Game Day Activity: Attend a Sporting Event

God's Key Play

Put on the full armor of God, so that you can
take your stand against the devil's schemes.
— EPHESIANS 6:11

Scouting Report for Dads

Congratulations! You did it. You made it to the Championship Game. All season long, you have been planning, executing, learning, applying, and growing in your relationships with your son and with God. My hope is that this has been a faith-stretching experience for you as well as for your son. You have fought the good fight and have made it to the final game of the season.

The old sports adage that defense wins championships was coined by legendary Alabama head coach Bear Bryant or a basketball coach from Minnesota, Dave Thorson. No matter who said it, I believe there is some truth to the phrase, especially as a Christian man in the 21st century. Some NFL analysts would argue that the times have turned in the league today—arguing that high-powered offenses win championships. While the stats may be starting to lean towards high-octane offenses, stay with me on the defense wins championship strategy concept for a few more minutes.

Throughout this season, you and your son have covered a variety of faith-stretching experiences. Have you noticed any themes? Have you noticed a common thread? Let's take a few minutes to review your season thus far.

We defined and discussed character and integrity. We then talked about work and money. Next, we learned how the Internet, pornography, and gaming could cause destruction and confusion in both our sons and ourselves. We then went on to learn the power of prayer in our lives and what kind of faith God wants us to have in Him. Jesus came to serve—so we showed our sons how we can serve just like Him. After serving, we learned the importance of having godly friends in our lives. Then we explored how to become content in the materialistic culture that we live in. During the last Game Day, we taught our sons how to properly treat the women in our lives and what it means to be an authentic man in God's eyes. Does anyone have a guess as to what theme runs throughout all games leading up to the championship game?

Can I give you a hint? It has to do with our opponent. During each Game Day, we have focused in on God's Word. We have gotten off of the bench, stepped onto the court, ran plays in from the sideline, walked between the ropes—you name it, we have done our best to teach our son how to become the man God intended him to be. We have done all of this out of true love for our sons. We try to spend as much time with our sons as we can. We try to balance our work life, our family life, our friend life, our spiritual life, and all of the other responsibilities we have in addition to being a father. We have done this because we have this innate desire to raise our sons to be better than ourselves. We would do anything for our sons—take away their pain, disease, sorrow, or loss. I believe most of us would lay our lives down for our sons.

There is only one problem—our opponent doesn't need to sleep. Our opponent doesn't have to balance all of the things we need to. Our opponent has only one job—to distract us away from God. Our opponent works 24/7 to lure our sons away from all that we can do as fathers to lead them to the true Father. So for today's Championship Game, we must prepare our sons and ourselves for battle. We must properly prepare for all that our opponent has to throw at us. And believe me, our opponent knows all of the trick plays, all of the decoys, and all of the ways to cheat the system without being caught.

Men, it's time to gear up for the Championship Game.

But before we gear up, I want to share one final story with you about an elite runner who broke a record, not by a mere tenth of a second, seconds, or minutes—in fact, not even by hours. Cliff Young won the Sydney to Melbourne Ultramarathon by almost two full days! When he showed up to compete against the other highly-trained professional marathoners with corporate sponsorship, Cliff showed up in a long-sleeved shirt, overalls, and gumboots.[1] Oh, by the way, Cliff was 61, had no formal training, and lived with his mom!

Cliff Young won the ultramarathon, not because of his performance-enhancing Under Armour outerwear, not because of his Nike running shoes, and certainly not because he was sponsored and tattooed with a corporate logo like today's athlete. Cliff Young won the ultramarathon because he had a different strategy.

At the start of the race, the professional runners left Cliff in the dust. Cliff steadily shuffled at slow speeds hour after hour. Cliff's strategy was to run straight through without sleeping. Cliff's competitors slept about six hours a night. Over time, Cliff slowly started gaining ground on the elite runners and eventually crossed the finish line in record time![2]

The reason I tell you this story is because advertising companies make us believe that if we don't wear Nike, Under Armour, Bauer, or Adidas, we won't be as competitive. While the technology of sportswear has certainly improved and Cliff Young might have been more comfortable at the end of his race, Cliff still won.

As we gear up for today's Championship Game, how do we prepare our sons and ourselves for Game Day? How do we prevent our sons and ourselves from running aimlessly or fighting like a boxer beating the air? How do we fight the good fight of faith and pursue righteousness, faith, love, endurance, and gentleness all while battling in God's name? The Championship Game depends on you passing this baton of information to your son. You must continually remind him of the lessons you both have learned in all of the games leading up to today's Game Day! You must model righteousness, godliness, faith, love, endurance, and gentleness in ALL that you do.

But, LaMaster, what is the secret to preparing for today's Championship Game? We have fought hard all season long. We have discussed some tough subjects that we have never before discussed. We have seen the Bible come to life throughout the last nine games. We have grown closer to each other and have stretched our faith in God.

I don't know if it is a secret, but one of the best illustrations to prepare your son for battle in today's Championship Game is to put on the Armor of God. Some of you may have heard of the Armor of God, and some of you may have read it. Take a few moments to read what Paul has to say in Ephesians 6:10–18:

> Finally, be strong in the Lord and in his mighty power. Put on the full armor of God, so that you can take your stand against the devil's schemes. For our struggle is not against flesh and blood, but against the rulers, against the authorities, against the powers of this dark world and against the spiritual forces of evil in the heavenly realms. Therefore, put on the *full armor of God*, so that when the day of evil comes, you may be able to stand your ground, and after you have done everything, to stand. Stand firm then, with the *belt of truth* buckled around your waist, with the *breastplate of righteousness* in place, and with your *feet* fitted with the readiness that comes from the *gospel of peace*. In addition to all this, take up the *shield of faith*, with which you can extinguish all the flaming arrows of the evil one. Take the *helmet of salvation* and the *sword of the Spirit*, which is the word of God. And *pray* in the Spirit on all occasions with all kinds of prayers and requests. With this in mind, be alert and always keep on praying for all the Lord's people.

Dads, it's time to break down the biggest defensive scheme of the season. Are you ready to help your son suit up for the Championship Game—with the full armor of God?

Pre-Game Planning

You know very well by now that I am a huge sports fan. You also know that I am an avid college football fan, in particular a die-hard Nebraska Cornhusker fan! I also know that many of you may be baseball fans or hockey fans. So I cannot think of a better way to illustrate the Armor of God than to use the metaphor of the protective equipment of football players, hockey goalies, and baseball catchers.

Many of us watch football August through February and read about the trades, deals, and off-season details from March through July. Some of us suited up in the pee-wee leagues, and some you may have even played college or professional football. You may be a fantasy football legend, or you may just enjoy watching the big game. Whatever your interest or lack of interest in football might be, when was the last time you really thought about all of the protective equipment (besides helmets) that football players must put on before running onto the field?

National Football League games begin in August and run through January. The National Hockey League season runs from early October through June. Finally, the Major League Baseball season starts in April and ends in October. I chose these three sports not only because they will help you illustrate the Armor of God to your son but also because the combination of the three seasons covers the entire year. Therefore, no matter what time of year you hold your Championship Game, you will be able to watch a game of football, hockey, or baseball.

When I watch football, hockey, or baseball, I rarely think of the protective equipment they are wearing. I am more interested in the score, the stats, and *SportsCenter* Top 10 Plays! Sure, with the recent rise in concussions, I have read a few articles about football helmets, but other than that, I don't give the uniforms much thought.

So I thought I would find out a little bit more about the protective gear worn by quarterbacks, goalies, and catchers—the most equipped players in their respective sports. Let's start with football.

NFL players range in weight from 150 to 360 pounds and in height from 5'5" to 6'9", bench-pressing up to 550 pounds. The fastest players run the 40-yard dash in as fast as 4.2 seconds.[3]

If that's not enough to frighten all of us fathers, consider the following research by Dr. Timothy Gay, professor of physics at the University of Nebraska (Go Big Red!). The average defensive back, weighing 199 pounds and running a 4.56-second 40-yard dash can produce up to 1,600 pounds of tackling force.[4]

The 2009 *Popular Mechanics* article by Matt Higgins goes on to expose more earth-shattering statistics. "Most people associate high g-forces with fighter pilots or astronauts. But common earthbound events can also boost g's. Few things can match the g-load of a wicked football hit."[4]

- Walking = 1 g
- Sneezing = 2.9 g
- Roller coaster = 5 g
- F-16 fighter jet roll = 9 g
- Concussion = 100 g
- Extreme football impact = 150 g

Higgins also mentions that despite the high-tech equipment in football today, there are "chinks in the armor." The human knee can withstand up to 500 pounds of pressure but is exposed to hits from the side and evasive maneuvers. In a three-year span, the NFL reported 1,200 knee injuries![4]

Hockey goalies must take on the 5.5-ounce, 1-inch thick, and 3-inch diameter piece of vulcanized rubber called the puck. It doesn't sound too intimidating until you find out that the world record speed of a slap shot is 110 mph, set by Denis Kulyash in 2011.[5] The goalie's equipment better not have any "chinks" in it. When the goalie is not worried about the puck, he must also evade the other players skating at average speeds of 29 mph.[6]

The fastest baseball pitch has been recorded at 105.1 mph (169.14 km/h) and was thrown by Aroldis Chapman (Cuba) for the Cincinnati Reds in a game against the San Diego Padres at PETCO Park, San Diego, California, on September 24, 2010.[7] Pitchers in MLB routinely throw the ball at speeds clocked in the high 90s. You can also picture at least one or two catcher collisions at home plate. Catchers can take a beating and must have the proper armor to protect their bodies.

Any guess on what it costs to outfit one Division 1 football player per year? Well, thanks to Tim Gardner of *USA Today*, we have our answer. According to Gardner, most Division 1 football programs spend more than $100,000 to outfit their team. "Add in practice gear, extra cleats, gloves, and other miscellaneous items, and Indiana University's annual cost tops $200,000."[8]

Broken down to a single player, you can see how the money piles up!

Football Player Armor[8]

- Helmet: $285
- Face mask: $20
- Mouth guard: $5
- Chin strap: $10
- Shoulder pads: $350
- Game jersey: $95
- Practice jersey: $40
- T-Shirts: $24 (2 shirts @ $12 each)
- Gloves: $200 (8 pairs @ $25/pair)
- Game pants: $85
- Practice pants: $40
- Knee brace: $1,200 (2 @ $600 each)
- Pant pads: $20
- Hex pad girdle: $32

- Shoes: $275 (5 pairs – 3 for practice, 2 styles for games – @ $55 each)
- Socks: $50 (10 pairs @ $5 each)

Total: $2,731

Well, that's a lot of cash. I do have one question for Gardner though—does the university get special deals on their cleats? Because I can't find a pair of Saucony's for work under 55 bucks!

The gear for a catcher in baseball might be a bit less expensive, but it is nothing to blink an eye at.

Baseball Catcher Armor

- Helmet: $100
- Chest protector: $100
- Leg guards: $100
- Catcher's mitt: $250
- Cleats: $125

Total: $675

Dads, if your son wants to become a goalie, I would encourage you to start saving now!

Hockey Goalie Armor

- Helmet/Mask: $1,000
- Helmet paint job: $750
- Stick: $80
- Chest and arm protectors: $300

- Leg protectors: $1,200
- Glove and blocker: $600
- Pants: $250
- Skates: $1,000

Total: $4,700

Now that we have reviewed the protective gear for quarterbacks, catchers, and goalies, let's talk about how much money it will cost us to outfit our sons and ourselves for the Championship Game.

The answer is easy—it costs $0! Zero. Nothing. Nada. Bupkis. Zilch.

The Armor of God costs us absolutely no money. Let's see how we can use a player's protective equipment to more easily illustrate the Armor of God to our sons.

Beginning in Ephesians 6:10, Paul tells us to be strong in the Lord and His mighty power. Then he instructs us to put on the full Armor of God so that we can stand up against the devil's schemes. As you can see, our defensive strategy for the Championship Game targets the devil's offensive schemes. There is no question who our opponent is; Paul states it very clearly.

Paul goes on to tell us that we must be ready and be dressed in full armor in preparation for the day when evil comes. Our preparation will allow us to stand our ground against our opponent.

The Armor of God is comprised of six pieces of protective gear: the belt of truth, the breastplate of righteousness, the shoes of peace, the shield of faith, the helmet of salvation, and the sword of the Spirit. Let's take a look at how the modern-day warrior (gridiron giants) can be used to illustrate the Armor of God in Ephesians 6.

Belt of Truth

Sports:

> Belts: Quarterbacks, goalies, and catchers wear belts to hold up their pants and pads and also for towels or hand warmers. Essentially, the belt is the foundation of the player's uniform. Without his belt, the player would lose his gear!

Armor of God:

> Paul's imagery of the belt of truth symbolizes God as our foundation for all. Without God, we are helpless, lonely, and vulnerable to the evil schemes of the devil. Armed with the belt of truth, we can defend ourselves from all that tempts us in this life—money, lust, materialism, greed, etc. Instead, the belt of truth helps keep our eyes on Him!

Breastplate of Righteousness

Sports:

> Shoulder Pads/Flak Jackets and Chest Protectors: The shoulder pads protect the player's shoulders and sternum area as well as their rotator cuff. Many quarterbacks wear a flak jacket to protect their ribs while they are throwing the ball. Chest protectors are vital for goalies and catchers to protect their sternum from the projectile pucks and baseball bullets that are fired at them. Essentially, the flak jackets and chest protectors are designed to protect the player's vital organs, including the heart, lungs, and abdomen.

Armor of God:

> At the time when Paul wrote Ephesians, the common belief was that the heart represented the mind and that the bowels represented emotions. Therefore, with the breastplate of righteousness, we are protecting our hearts and minds from the devil's schemes. Righteousness comes from Jesus Christ. We cannot become righteous through our own good works. We must put on the breastplate of righteousness and live with our eyes fixed on Him!

Gospel of Peace (Shoes)

Sports:

> Cleats/Skates: The cleats are worn for traction and foot and ankle support. Cleats come in various lengths and are chosen based on the type of field and field conditions on game day. Football equipment managers typically pack three types of cleats for each game to ensure the players have the best traction on the field. Goalie skates have added padding and protection as well as a non-curved blade for better lateral motion on the ice.

Armor of God:

> Paul tells us to fit our feet with the readiness that comes with the gospel of peace. Picture soldiers in sandals marching through the unpaved roads of Rome. The right sandals would help protect the soldiers' feet from the elements as well as stabilizing them on their long marches and during battle. Paul knew that the stability from the sandals was key to a soldier's uniform. Where does our stability come from? God's Word. God's Word gives us stability by providing knowledge and protection from the enemy. The devil has set tricks and traps for each of us and will continue to throughout our lives.

By equipping ourselves with the gospel of peace, we can overcome these tricks and traps.

Shield of Faith

Sports:
> Pads: The quarterback, catcher, and goalie all wear multiple pads that shield them from the dangers of their chosen game. These include pads specifically designed to protect other body parts: thigh pads, hip pads, tail pads, neck rolls, knee pads, elbow pads, leg protectors, chin guards, mouth guards, and throat guards, to name a few.

Armor of God:
> When I think of a Roman soldier in Paul's era, I first think of their shield (or *Scutum*).[9] These massive shields weighed 22 pounds and were 41.5 inches high, 16 inches across, and 12 inches deep (due to its semi-cylindrical shape). Placed side by side, Roman soldiers could protect themselves from swords, arrows, and other weapons. The shield was the soldier's best tool for protection. The shield of faith is just as important to the Armor of God. The shield of faith gives us God's strength and protection—strength in knowledge and confidence as well as protection from the devil's doubts, lies, and temptations he shoots at us.

Helmet of Salvation

Sports:
> Helmet and Facemask: The helmet protects or minimizes the risk of head trauma such as concussions. The facemask protects the player's eyes, nose, and mouth from injury.

Armor of God:

One hit to the head can incapacitate even the most highly trained soldier. Roman soldiers' helmets were essential to survival during the hand-to-hand battles they experienced. As we put on the helmet of salvation for the Armor of God, we are protected from the devil's hell and promised an eternal life in God's heaven. If we go into battle without our helmets, we leave ourselves vulnerable to the evil plans of the devil. Keep your helmet of salvation on at all times.

Sword of the Spirit

Sports:

The quarterback's sword is his throwing arm. The baseball catcher's sword is his bat. The goalie's sword is his stick. These are all offensive tools for the player and are used to help their team win the game.

Armor of God:

All other pieces of the Armor of God have been used for defense. Paul included the sword of the Spirit as the only offensive piece in the Armor of God. When our belief and faith in Jesus Christ is challenged, we need an offensive weapon to combat these challenges. The Holy Spirit is our tool of choice and is the final piece of the Armor of God. The Holy Spirit guides us with the word of the Gospel, leading us along His path. Hebrews 4:12 illustrates the power of God's Word: "For the word of God is alive and active. Sharper than any double-edged sword, it penetrates even to dividing soul and spirit, joints and marrow; it judges the thoughts and attitudes of the heart."

Paul wraps up his illustration of the Armor of God with prayer. In fact, he tells us to pray on all occasions for all of His people. For today's Championship Game, you and your son will be attending a sporting event and learning all about the Armor of God.

Pre-Game Day Prayer

Dear Heavenly Father,

We thank You for all that we have learned from You in our season so far! _____ (Your son's name) and I continue to grow closer to each other as well as closer to You because of our time together, our time in Your Word, and because of Your grace. As we begin our Championship Game, _____ (your son's name) and I pray for safe travels to and from the game, for focus on Your word, for true understanding of Your Armor, and for the ability to share what we have learned with others. Help me to teach _____ (your son's name) how to "gear up" in the Armor of God as Paul so eloquently instructed us to do nearly 2,000 years ago. I pray that the illustration of the protective equipment of today's athlete helps _____ (your son's name) to identify the protection You have graciously given every person that believes in You—all for free. I pray that the Holy Spirit guides me today as I instruct my son towards You.
In Jesus' name we pray, Amen.

Playbook

One of my favorite memories with my dad is when we went to the Nebraska versus Oklahoma football game. I was a freshman at the University of

Nebraska, my dad's alma mater. It was the day after Thanksgiving, November 23, 1993. The wind chill was well below zero, snow was lightly falling, and our Huskers were rated number 1, while Oklahoma was rated number 15. It has since become a Big Eight classic, full of big names and big plays and would lead to an undefeated season. Tom Osborne's Huskers were led by quarterback Tommie Frazier (Heisman finalist), Trev Alberts (Butkus winner), running back Calvin Jones, and defensive back Mike Minter.

With full winter gear on, my dad and I watched every play of the game from the sixth row in the student section. With hot chocolate to help warm us, we dined on Runzas and red hot dogs (Fairbury Reds) as we watched Nebraska beat their long-time rival, the Sooners, 21–7. We not only saw a great rivalry game but we bonded as father and son and made a memory that I can go back to in an instant. I can still feel the bitterly cold wind on my face and the warmth of the hot chocolate, and I can see the exact play when Trev Alberts hurt his shoulder. There is something about going to a game as father and son that brings you closer together.

For today's Championship Game, you and your son will attend a football game, baseball game, or hockey game. I would encourage you to make plans to attend either a professional or Division 1 college game. That being said, I know that tickets, travel, and time may be limited for some of you. There are many semi-pro teams, such as AAA baseball teams, USHL hockey teams, and indoor or arena football teams across the country that will work just as well.

Here is a list of what you will need to do for the Championship Game:

1. Select a date when you and your son can attend a football, hockey, or baseball game. Make sure it doesn't conflict with other pre-planned family activities!
2. Talk with your son to see what type of game he wants to attend.
3. Work with your son to plan and budget for the game. Remember to include the cost of tickets, fuel, food, and souvenirs. If your trip

requires that you stay overnight, don't forget to include the cost of the hotel or motel.

4. Purchase tickets for your selected game. You can find tickets directly through the program's website, via Stubhub.com, or even through Craigslist.com.

5. Both of you will need to read Ephesians 6:10–18. Have your son identify and write down the equipment Paul identifies in the Armor of God. He can do this while you are on your way to the game.

6. Review and have your son read the Cliff Young story. Talk about this on your commute to the game.

7. While on your way to the game, explain to your son that the purpose of the Championship Game is to describe the Armor of God and how the protective equipment of a football, hockey, or baseball player can help illustrate the armor that God has for us.

8. Before you leave, study and review the Pre-Game Planning section so you can comfortably talk through each piece of the Armor of God with your son while you are driving to the big game.

9. During the game, examine the protective equipment of the players, and have your son compare that to each piece of the Armor of God. He will most likely need some help, so don't forget to take this book into the game with you as a reference.

10. If possible, either before or after the game, see if you can get down near the field or ice to see the players up close. I usually sit in the nosebleed section and know that this distorts the actual size of these massive athletes. Providing the opportunity for your son to see the size of the players at eyelevel will help with the impact of this lesson. (It might also allow you the opportunity for an autograph or two.)

Materials you will need:
- FNL4FS book
- Pen and paper
- Bible

- Binoculars (if you have them)
- Smartphone or video camera
- Snacks and drinks for the road trip
- Sharpie pen for autographs (optional)

Post-Game Day Analysis

I hope your team won the big game! I also hope that you and your son have a greater appreciation for the Armor of God. As we enter into the Post-Game Day Analysis of the Championship Game, I suggest that you and your son find a favorite restaurant or hang out to fully analyze the game. Depending on drive time, you may need to get on the road sooner than later, but I encourage you to take just a few minutes to answer the following questions as well as a few more minutes to record the Post-Game Press Conference media questions. This would be tough and dangerous to do while driving.

1. Do you have a better understanding of the Armor of God? Why?
2. How does the devil try to trick, tempt, or lie to you? Give at least one example.
3. Can you name all of the pieces of the Armor of God?
4. What are your thoughts on brand names after hearing the story of Cliff Young? What is the moral or meaning of the Cliff Young story?
5. Do you think you could share the Armor of God with your brothers, sisters, or friends? If so, who would you like to share it with first and why?
6. Which piece of the Armor of God is used for offense? Explain.

Post-Game Day Press Conference

Media Questions for Dad

Have your son start recording and ask you the following questions:

1. For the record, what game did we go to, who played, and what was the final score?
2. What was your favorite play of the game today?
3. Dad, what piece of the Armor of God do you need to strengthen?
4. As of today, what is your strongest piece of Armor?
5. Dad, what do you think is my strongest piece in the Armor of God?

Media Questions for Your Son

Start recording and ask your son the following questions:

1. _____ (Your son's name), what was your favorite play of the game today?
2. What was the most important thing you learned about the Armor of God today?
3. What do you think is the most important piece in the Armor of God and why?
4. How would you rate today's Championship Game? Circle the helmets below (1 helmet = Not so good and 5 helmets = Awesome)

Link's X's and O's

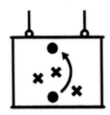

X: I love going to games with my dad! I love hanging out with my family, but sometimes you just need dad and son time.

O: I am ready to gear up in the Armor of God. Who's with me?

Post-Game Day Prayer

Dear Heavenly Father,

We are so thankful for the amazing season that we have had together focusing on Your Word! I am amazed at how much _____ (your son's name) has grown spiritually. I am also amazed at how much closer he and I have grown together as father and son. For that, I want to thank You, Lord. I know that You designed me to instruct _____ (your son's name) towards You and Your Word. I stand in awe of what I have learned about Your Word and am so thankful for every second that I have spent with _____ (your son's name). I pray that this is only the beginning of improving our father and son journey as well as our journey to glorify You and to spread Your Word.

In Jesus' name we pray, Amen.

Do you not know that in a race all the runners run, but only one gets the prize? Run in such a way as to get the prize. Everyone who competes in the games goes into strict training. They do it to get a crown that will not last, but we do it to get a crown that will last forever. Therefore I do not run like someone running aimlessly; I do not fight like a boxer beating the air. No, I strike a blow to my body and make it my slave so that after I have preached to others, I myself will not be disqualified for the prize.
— 1 CORINTHIANS 9:24–27

Post-Season

The best things your children will learn about God will be from watching you try to find out for yourself. Jesus said, "Seek and you will find." They will not always do what you tell them to do, but they will be—good and bad—as they see you being. If your children see you seeking, they will seek—the finding part is up to God.

— *P. Berrian Berends*

FNL4FS Award Ceremony

ust when you thought the season was wrapping up, you get an email from your son's coach that informs you of the award ceremony. I have to be honest, at the end of a sports season, I look forward to having an open evening, even if it is only for a couple of weeks between seasons.

But alas, you pack up the family in the car and head to the award ceremony. I have noticed that all award ceremonies can be broken down into three main parts:

- The video slideshow
- The guest speaker
- The trophy or award distribution

"Ceremonies are those special occasions that weave the fabric of human existence." Robert Lewis goes on to remind us to "Think back upon the significant moments in your life. With few exceptions, the value of those moments was sealed by ceremonies." In his book, *Raising a Modern-Day Night*, Lewis highlights the impact of ceremonies on a young boy's life. "Ceremony should be one of the crown jewels for helping a boy become a man."[1]

Well, I hereby announce the plan for the FNL4FS Award Ceremony. This is a special time for you and your son, but it will take some time and effort from both of you to make it memorable. This can be a family affair, but I would also encourage you to invite grandparents, aunts and uncles, cousins, your pastor, and friends to share in your championship season celebration.

Here is the agenda for the *Friday Night Lights for Fathers and Sons* Award Ceremony:

- Press Conference Video Compilation
- Reading of "The Letters"
- Award (Not Trophies) Presentation

Without further ado, let's start preparing for the FNL4FS Award Ceremony!

Press Conference Video Compilation

Dad: It's time to get your smartphone or video camera out and review all of the Post-Game Press Conference video footage. For the Press Conference Video Compilation (PCVC), you will need to use a video software program such as Windows Movie Maker or Apple iMovie. There are certainly other software programs available, but these are probably the most well known and most user friendly.

You may need to enlist the help of someone that is more technologically versed than you are. Don't be afraid to ask for help; this is one of the keys to the PCVC. You most likely know someone that has worked with video editing before.

- Option 1: Compile all video footage without editing. Then burn the movie onto a DVD.
- Option 2: Edit the video footage for the highlights with a target of 15–20 minutes. Then burn it onto a DVD.

Make sure you back up the video footage onto your computer's hard drive, back up drive, or flash drive. We don't want these precious videos to disappear. I recommend the DVD for both options because both you and your son can have a portable copy of this forever!

Be as creative as you want to be with the video. Here are a few ideas to get your creative juices flowing:

- Personalized DVD jacket cover
- Add your son's favorite music
- A personalized video introduction to honor your son
- Add video from your wife, your daughter, your friends, your pastor, your son's friends, or your son's grandparents. This is a great touch, especially if they are not able to make it to the award ceremony.
- Add in pictures of you and your son:
  - The day of his birth
  - His first day of school
  - His baptism
  - Other significant events
- Favorite Bible verses

These are just a few examples, but I know that many of you are much more creative and innovative than I am. I would love to see clips from your PCVCs, not just for me but also for all of the dads going through a 10-game season with their sons. If you would like, please share your video clips at the Friday Night Lights for Fathers and Sons Facebook page.

As you are creating this timeless memory, don't get discouraged and frustrated. Remember that the finished product will be a treasure for both you and your son.

Once you have completed the Post Conference Video Collection, it will be time to prepare "The Letters."

"The Letters"

For Dads

I am continually amazed at how Nebraska Football is interwoven in the relationship I have with my dad. I truly believe that this lifelong connection is one of the reasons I was led to write this book with a sports theme.

In 2006 the University of Nebraska added new seats in the north end of Memorial Stadium. In doing so, they announced a lottery for those interested in season tickets. I told my dad that I had entered my name into the lottery. My dad, with a little bit of a "Debbie Downer" tone, told me that he wasn't going to waste his time because the only people that got tickets were people that gave big donations. Well, "Debbie Downer" didn't deter me, and later that summer, the University of Nebraska Ticket Office called me and informed me that I had been randomly drawn for two season tickets! Before they asked if I would like them, I told the ticket agent that I would purchase them immediately!

In the early fall, I received a letter in the mail. It was in a standard white envelope with a postmark from my hometown. I eagerly opened the envelope and found a one-page, handwritten letter from my dad. Here is an abbreviated version of the letter:

Dear Mark,

Thank you so much for taking the chance at getting the Nebraska season tickets. I'm so proud of you for going for something you wanted. We sure have a lot of good memories ahead of us that now will also include "Go Big Red" games.... I love you, Mark, and I'm very proud of the man and father and husband that you've become.

Love,
Dad

That was nine years ago, and I still have this letter. I happen upon it every once in a while, and it still makes me get goosebumps. My dad and I don't always talk like this. It's not often that my dad tells me that he is proud of the man, father, and husband that I've become, but he doesn't need to. I know how he feels because he told me in a handwritten letter. It doesn't matter to me that he wrote it nine years ago. I still know what his heart feels.

I know I am not alone in craving this type of feedback from my father. I can almost guarantee that the handwritten letter you will be writing to your son will be something that he will keep for his entire life. He will cherish the letter. He will read it when he needs encouragement, strength, and reassurance. He will hold onto it tightly after you have gone to heaven, knowing that the letter is one of his closest connections he has to you, your heart, and your mind. Your penmanship alone may bring him to tears.

Kent Nerburn wrote a book entitled *Letters to My Son: A Father's Wisdom on Manhood, Life, and Love*. As with many of us, the birth of our son changed our perspective on life. Nerburn shares a collection of letters he wrote to his son with chapters including "Strength," "Work," "Money and Wealth," "The Spiritual Journey," "Falling in Love," and, of course, "Fatherhood." Before I even began writing this book, I knew that a letter to my son would be an integral part of the package—directly inspired by Nerburn and his book, *Letters to My Son*.[2]

The words we write to our sons are powerful, long lasting, and inspiring. A handwritten letter is not an email that you delete immediately after reading it. The personality reflected in the penmanship is invisible if the letter is typed. Phone calls or conversations are not typically recorded. A handwritten letter implies that the person writing has taken the time to focus his thoughts directly on the receiver of the letter.

Are you ready to write your letter? Here is a sample letter to get you started.

Date (DD/MM/YYYY)

Dear _____ (your son's name),

. The past 10 Game Days have been some of the best days of my life. I am so blessed to have you as a son. You are an amazing and talented boy who is growing into a wonderful young man right in front of my eyes. God truly gave me a gift when he brought you into my life.

Because of our time together, I feel that we have both grown closer to God. I have learned so much from you, and I can only hope that you have learned much from me. _____ (Your son's name), God has an amazing plan for you. He has blessed you with _____ (list out your son's talents here). You can do anything that you put your mind to.

Please know that I pray for you every single day. I pray for your future, your health, your protection, our relationship, your relationship with God, your friends, your future spouse, and your future children. Most of all, I pray that you put God first in your life.

_____ (Your son's name), you will go through good times and bad times in life. During both the good and bad times, fix your eyes on God. He is always with you.

Over the last 10 Game Days, my favorite memory was

_____ .

My favorite Game Day was Game Day # _____ because_____ .

My favorite Bible verse from the Game Days was _____ because _____ .

I knew you understood the meaning of Game Day # _____
when you _____ .

_____ (Your son's name), I am so proud to be your father. My life is better because you are in it. Know that you can always come to me to talk about anything. Believe me, I have most likely experienced anything you might have questions about.

I love you _____ (your son's name)! I am proud of the boy you are and of the young man you are becoming. God bless you always.

Love,
Dad

Please know that this is only a sample to get you started and to give you ideas of what to write to your son. Take some time thinking about what you are going to write about. The ideas will start coming, and they will keep on coming. Make sure you are in a quiet area and have minimal distractions when writing the letter.

Know that you will be reading this letter to your son (yes, out loud) in front of all the attendees of the award ceremony. By both reading and writing this letter, you will have a profound impact on your son.

For Sons
Next, have your son write you a letter. This might be something that his mother, a sibling, or a friend can help him write. Here are a few ideas to help him get started writing the letter:

- What was your favorite Game Day and why?
- What Bible verse meant the most to you?
- What is your favorite memory from the 10 Game Days and why?

- Tell your dad what he taught you about becoming closer to God.
- Tell your dad that you love him.
- Tell your dad that you enjoy spending time with him and want to spend more time with him.
- Share some ideas on what you and your dad could do together in the future.
- What is your favorite part about spending time with your dad?
- Remember to use your best penmanship when writing the letter to your dad.
- Remember to write the full date and year on the letter.
- The letter only needs to be a page long, but you can write more if you would like.
- Be creative. Draw a picture of your favorite memory or Game Day.
- Make a paper airplane out of the letter you wrote after you read it to your dad.
- Remember that you will be reading this letter out loud to your dad and everyone that is at the award ceremony!

Finally, if anyone would be willing to share their letters or parts of their letters with the rest of the FNL4FS fathers, please go to the Friday Night Lights for Fathers and Sons Facebook page and share.

Award (Not Trophy) Presentation

The Award (Not Trophy) Presentation is to be the culmination of you and your son's 10-game season journey through this *Friday Night Lights for Fathers and Sons* book. So far, the Award Ceremony has been made up of memorable moments marked by video memories and spoken and written words of affirmation. While the DVD and "The Letters" will most likely be packed away in safe storage and pulled out from time to time, I would like to suggest an award that is a constant reminder of you and your son's FNL4FS experience.

No, the award is not a trophy, although you both deserve a trophy because you earned it and did not just participate! No, it is not a picture of the two of you together during one of your Game Days. And no, it is not a football, baseball, or hockey puck to symbolize your Championship Game experience. While these are all great ideas for you to get for your son, I have created something that both of you can wear every day as a constant reminder of your FNL4FS experience, your father and son relationship, and your reliance on your Father God.

I have created a unique FNL4FS memory band for you to present to your son during the Award (Not Trophy) Presentation. This silicone wristband includes FNL4FS on one side and Ephesians 6:11 on the other side. I have included a football icon on the FNL4FS side and a cross and shield on the Ephesians 6:11 side.

Here is a sample script you can use to present the FNL4FS memory band to your son.

_____ (Your son's name), as you have successfully completed the Friday Night Lights for Fathers and Sons 10-Game Season, I would like to present you with the Friday Night Lights for Fathers and Sons memory band.

Show the memory band to your son and those that are at the award ceremony.

I would like to explain what the memory band symbolizes:

FNL4FS: This symbolizes our time together during the 10-game FNL4FS season. It represents all of the memories we shared with everyone tonight, "The Letters," and all of the memories we shared together during our Game Days.

Football: The football represents our love of sports and how we can use sports to grow closer together as well as closer to God.

Ephesians 6:11: This Bible verse will serve as a constant reminder that we should "Put on the full armor of God, so that you can take your stand against the devil's schemes." The full Armor of God includes the following: 1) the Belt of Truth, 2) the Breastplate of Righteousness, 3) the Gospel of Peace (Shoes), 4) the Shield of Faith, 5) the Helmet of Salvation, and 6) The Sword of the Spirit. Gear Up for God!

Cross: The cross represents our belief in Jesus Christ; that He is the son of God; that He died on the cross to forgive our sins; and that He promises us eternal life.

Shield: The shield represents the Shield of Faith and reminds us to always have faith in God.

Memory Band: The memory band represents the bond between you and me as father and son.

At this time, place the memory band on your son's wrist. Then state the following:

The FNL4FS memory band also represents the bond that we have with other fathers and sons that have completed the 10-game FNL4FS season.

Now take out your FNL4FS memory band and have your son place it on your wrist.

It might be the perfect time to have someone snap a few pictures of you and your son exchanging memory bands.

Well, that about does it for the FNL4FS Award Ceremony. As I have mentioned several times in the past, I would love to hear from you about your

Award Ceremony on the Friday Night Lights for Fathers and Sons Facebook page. Feel free to share pictures, videos, ideas, suggestions, etc., for all of the other fathers and sons that are at the beginning, middle, or end of their season. Your post may also inspire other dads to take on the FNL4FS season!

I have a vision of walking in a public place and running into another father and son wearing the FNL4FS memory band. Can you imagine how cool that would be? Or better yet, what if you and your son started wearing the FNL4FS memory bands to church, football practice, basketball practice, band practice, Trail Life meetings, work, or any other activities where other dads could ask you about them. Perhaps you could start a small group in your church and help guide other dads and sons closer to God through FNL4FS.

If you are interested in purchasing the FNL4FS memory band for yourself and your son, you can do so at my website: marklamaster.com. I have made them reasonably priced and have sizes that will fit both you and your son.

Post-Season Self-Scouting Survey

Last but not least, the time has come to take the Post-Season version of the Self-Scouting Survey. My hope is that each of you have grown closer in both your relationship with your son and your relationship with God over the past 10 Game Days. Take a few moments to complete the Post-Season Self-Scouting Survey below.

Please circle the answer that best describes you as the dad you are today.

1. During the typical weekday, I spend an average of _____ with my son.
    a. between 30 and 60 minutes
    b. greater than 2 hours
    c. less than 30 minutes
    d. between 1 and 2 hours

2. During a typical weekend, I spend an average of _____ with my son.
   a. between 1 and 2 hours
   b. greater than 4 hours
   c. less than 1 hour
   d. between 2 and 4 hours

3. I tuck my son into bed an average of _____ nights per week.
   a. 3–5
   b. 6–7
   c. 0–1
   d. 1–3

4. The last time I said, "I love you," to my son was _____ .
   a. yesterday
   b. today
   c. I can't remember
   d. last month

5. The most recent time I prayed with my son was _____ .
   a. last week
   b. last night
   c. I can't remember
   d. last month

6. When was the last time you planned an event or activity with just you and your son?
   a. last month
   b. last week
   c. never
   d. last year

7. When my son needs help with homework, I _____ .
   a. usually help him

    b.   stop what I am doing and help him

    c.   have his mom, brother, or sister help him

    d.   try to help him but then get distracted or frustrated

8.   I carve out time in my day to talk to my son about his concerns related to friend issues, expected body changes, and other difficult topics:

    a.   I schedule time a couple of times a year.

    b.   I both schedule time and take time to talk to him as situations arise.

    c.   I let his mother handle those things.

    d.   I have tried this several times, but I am just not good at this kind of stuff.

9.   I take my family to church _____ .

    a.   about 2 times per month

    b.   every Sunday, with rare exceptions

    c.   on Easter and Christmas Eve

    d.   several times per year between my son's sports seasons

10.   I read the Bible _____ .

    a.   a few days a week

    b.   every day

    c.   rarely, if ever

    d.   once a month, maybe

Count up all of the d's you circled, and enter that number next to the letter below. Then do the same for the c's, b's, and a's.

d _____ c _____ b_____ a_____

All right, now for the moment of truth. Determine which letter you have the most of, and circle the letter below to determine the type of dad you are now. After reading this book and going through the 10-Game season with your son, did you become a Playoff Dad?

B. Playoff Dad

Strong work! I knew you could do it. If you were a Playoff Dad during your first survey, keep it up and share your strategies with other dads! I would love to hear from you on how you became a Playoff Dad!

A. Starting Lineup Dad

Congratulations! You have made the starting lineup, Dad! With continued focus, intention, and action, you will make the playoffs soon.

D. 6th Man Dad

You are on the right track! You have earned your spot to become the first man off the bench! I hope that you have found several resources in the 10-Game season to work your way towards the playoffs.

C. Benchwarmer Dad

No worries, Dad! The fact that you are reading this book shows me that you want to become a better dad. It is not impossible to move up to the 6th Man, Starting Lineup, or Playoff Dad categories. With continued prayer, sacrifice, and commitment to your son, you will make the changes you and your son need.

Off-Season Planning

---

*But you, man of God, flee from all this, and pursue
righteousness, godliness, faith, love, endurance and
gentleness. Fight the good fight of faith. Take hold of
eternal life to which you were called when you made
your good confession in the presence of many witnesses.*

— 1 TIMOTHY 6:11–12

Congratulations! You have completed a winning season as a father and son team! You have strengthened your father–son relationship and have improved your relationship with your Father God. Now that you have completed your 10-game winning season of *Friday Night Lights for Fathers and Sons*, I strongly encourage you to continue strengthening your relationship with your son and with God.

What are some of the things that were season-changing for you and your son? Was there one key play or Game Day that determined the outcome of the season for either of you? What is one area that you and your son improved in this season? Your relationship with God? Your understanding of your son's friendships? Or is it that you and your son now talk more freely than you did before? Did either of you find a new activity that you can do together that you did not do before the season? Did you try something new that this book suggested and it has now become part of your weekly or monthly routine? Have you become more involved with new friends, the church, service projects, or money talks now that you have read this book?

Lyrics to the JJ Weeks Band song "Let Them See You":

> Does the man I am today say the words You need to say?
> Let them see You in me let them hear You when I speak
> Let them feel You when I sing
> Let them see You, let them see You in me
> Who am I without Your grace, another smile another face
> Another breath a grain of sand passing quickly through Your hand
> I give my life an offering take it all take everything[1]

Are you the man you want to be today? Are you the father that you want to be today? I believe that by simply asking yourself this question, you are on your way to becoming a better man and a better father. For more inspiration, I turn to one of my favorite authors on the topic, Steve Farrar.

Steve Farrar is one of my favorite authors on what it means to be a Christian man and father. Farrar started writing about Christian men when others weren't even thinking about it. At the age of 40, Farrar wrote *Point Man: How a Man Can Lead His Family*. Mind you, men's ministries were virtually non-existent when his book was published in 1990. I consider Farrar the father of Christian men-specific books. I had the privilege of hearing Steve Farrar speak at the 2015 No Regrets Men's Conference. His message convinced me to continue on with writing this book—for which I will be forever grateful. On a final note, Farrar's vulnerability about becoming a writer also helped me during the times when the Spirit did not guide my words onto my laptop for this book. In the introduction of *Point Man*, Farrar admits to having "stuck" days in which he could simply not write. He stated that these became the days he was most fond of because he would talk to God and find answers.[2] You will have to read *Point Man* to find out what he asked God!

Farrar's request was granted and resonated with men all over the world. In another of Farrar's books, *King Me: What Every Son Wants and Needs from His Father*, he offers one of the best biblical definitions of fatherhood that I have found. Can any of you guess where this might come from? I am guessing that most of you would not have guessed Deuteronomy. I know that this may seem like a book way out in left field or not on the field at all, but stay with Farrar and me for a few paragraphs.

Farrar states that Deuteronomy 6:5–7 contains a job description for fathers. To simplify this, Farrar says that the Bible cites two job responsibilities for fathers:

- Love God Deeply
- Teach Your Son Diligently[3]

Here is Deuteronomy 6:5–7 to help give you a sense of where Farrar is getting this fatherhood job description:

> Love the LORD your God with all your heart and with all your soul and with all your strength. These commandments that I give you today are to be on your hearts. Impress them on your children. Talk about them when you sit at home and when you walk along the road, when you lie down and when you get up.

Farrar goes on to write, with emphasis, the following statement: "Fathers were meant to be present in the lives of their sons, and they were to be very intentional in their presence."[3]

We must be present and intentional in the lives of our sons. Completing the 10-game season was only a start. For some of you, you still have 10 years left to teach your son how to love God deeply and teach your son diligently. For others, you may only have a few years left. Our time on the field is limited. The clock is ticking. Tick. How will you spend the remaining years you have with your son? Tock.

Tick. Tock. The clock is counting down. Now is the time to focus on you and your son's relationship, your son's relationship with God, and your relationship with God.

Tick, tock. Tick, tock. Tick, tock...

Fatherhood Personnel Files

Every Young Man's Battle: Strategies for Victory in the Real World of Sexual Temptation, Stephen Arterburn and Fred Stoeker

Papa's Blessings: The Gift That Keeps Giving—A Step-by-Step Guide to Developing and Bestowing a Blessing upon Those Who Matter in Your Life, Greg Bourgond

PlayStation Nation: Protect Your Child from Video Game Addiction, Olivia and Kurt Bruner

Heaven Is for Real: A Little Boy's Astounding Story of His Trip to Heaven and Back, Todd Burpo

The 21-Day Dad's Challenge: Three Weeks to a Better Relationship with Your Kids, Carey Casey (ed.)

Bringing Up Boys: Shaping the Next Generation of Men, James Dobson

Wild at Heart: Discovering the Secret of a Man's Soul, John Eldredge

King Me: What Every Son Wants and Needs from His Father, Steve Farrar

Point Man: How a Man Can Lead His Family, Steve Farrar

Six Ways to Keep the "Good" in Your Boy: Guiding Your Son from His Tweens to His Teens, Dannah Gresh

Do Hard Things: A Teenage Rebellion Against Low Expectations, Alex and Brett Harris

Too Busy Not to Pray: Slowing Down to Be with God, Bill Hybels

Better Dads, Stronger Sons: How Fathers Can Guide Boys to Become Men of Character, Rick Johnson

Men's Fraternity: The Quest for Authentic Manhood, Robert Lewis

Raising a Modern-Day Knight: A Father's Role in Guiding His Son to Authentic Manhood, Robert Lewis

Boys Should Be Boys: 7 Secrets to Raising Healthy Sons, Meg Meeker

The Dad in the Mirror: How to See Your Heart for God Reflected in Your Children, Patrick Morley and David Delk

Letters to My Son: A Father's Wisdom on Manhood, Life, and Love, Kent Nerburn

Passport2Purity Getaway Kit by FamilyLife—Version 3, Dennis and Barbara Rainey

The Total Money Makeover: A Proven Plan for Financial Fitness, Dave Ramsey
Smart Money Smart Kids: Raising the Next Generation to Win with Money, Dave Ramsey and Rachel Cruze

ENDNOTES

Preseason

Introduction

1. Lewis, R. (2006). *Winning at Work & Home: Authentic Manhood*. Nashville, Tenn.: LifeWay Press.
2. Spock, B., & Rothenberg, M. (1985). *Baby and Child Care* (Rev. and updated ed.). New York: E.P. Dutton.
3. Dodson, F. (1970). *How to Parent*. Los Angeles: Nash Pub.
4. Dodson, F. (1974). *How to Father*. Los Angeles: Nash Pub.
5. Amazon.com: Books. (n.d.). Retrieved September 5, 2015.

Chapter 2

1. Vespa, J., Lewis, J., & Kreider, R. (2013, August 1). America's Families and Living Arrangements: 2012. Retrieved June 1, 2015, from http://www.census.gov/prod/2013pubs/p20-570.pdf
2. United States Census Bureau. (2010, November 1). Retrieved June 1, 2015, from http://www.census.gov/population/www/socdemo/hh-fam/cps2010.html
3. Sisarich, T. (Director). (2014). *Irreplaceable* [Motion picture].
4. Farrar, S. (2005). *King Me*. Chicago: Moody.
5. Brewster, D. (2005, August 1). The "4/14 Window"; Child Ministries and Mission Strategies. Retrieved June 5, 2015, from http://www.compassion.com/multimedia/The 4_14 Window.pdf
6. Low, R. (2003). The Truth about Men and the Church. Retrieved September 24, 2014, from http://www.touchstonemag.com/archives/article.php?id=16-05-024-v#ixzz3mhTqhNz4

Regular Season

Game Day 1

1. Devlin, D. (Director). (2000). *The Patriot* [Motion picture on DVD]. Columbia TriStar Home Video.
2. John Wooden's greatest quotes. (2010, June 5). Retrieved June 7, 2015, from http://sports.espn.go.com/ncb/news/story?id=5249709
3. Inspirational Quote of the day: C.S. Lewis. (n.d.). Retrieved June 7, 2015, from http://www.inspirationalwords365.com/inspirational-quote-of-the-day-c-s-lewis/

Game Day 2

1. The Bible and Money – Church Curriculum. (2015). Retrieved September 5, 2015.
2. Alcorn, R. (2001). *The Treasure Principle*. Sisters, Or.: Multnomah.
3. Ramsey, D. & Cruze, R. (2014). Work: It's Not a Four-Letter Word. In *Smart Money Smart Kids: Raising the Next Generation to Win with Money* (p. 18). Thomas Nelson Pub.
4. Ramsey, D. & Cruze, R. (2014). Spend: When It's Gone, It's Gone. In *Smart Money Smart Kids: Raising the Next Generation to Win with Money* (pp. 48–49). Thomas Nelson Pub.
5. Ramsey, D. (2003). *The Total Money Makeover: A Proven Plan for Financial Fitness*. Nashville: Thomas Nelson Pub.
6. Bible Gateway passage: Matthew 25:15 – New International Version. (2015). Retrieved June 10, 2015, from https://www.biblegateway.com/passage/?search=Matthew25:15&version=NIV

Game Day 3

1. Pawloski, A. (2014, September 18). Meet the Teen Whose Life Was Almost Ruined by Internet Addiction. Retrieved September 5, 2015, from http://www.today.com/parents/secret-life-teens-internet-addiction-changes-boy-shell-son-1D80153806

2. Zimbardo, P. (2011, March 1). The Demise of Guys? | TED Talk | TED.com. Retrieved August 5, 2015, from http://www.ted.com/talks/zimchallenge

3. Zimbardo, P. & Duncan, N. (2012). *The Demise of Guys: Why Boys Are Struggling and What We Can Do about It*. New York: TED Conferences.

4. Cleave, R. (2010). *Unplugged: My Journey into the Dark World of Video Game Addiction*. Deerfield Beach, FL: Health Communications.

5. Wilson, G. (2015). *Your Brain on Porn: Internet Pornography and the Emerging Science of Addiction*. Margate: Commonwealth Publishing.

6. Bruner, O. & Bruner, K. (2006). *PlayStation Nation: Protect Your Child from Video Game Addiction*. New York: Center Street.

7. Roberts, K. (2010). *Cyber Junkie: Escape the Gaming and Internet Trap*. Center City, Minn.: Hazelden.

8. Gilkerson, L. (2010, August 19). Teens and Porn: 10 Stats You Need to Know. Retrieved August 7, 2015, from http://www.covenanteyes.com/2010/08/19/teens-and-porn-10-stats-your-need-to-know/

9. Katehakis, A. (2011, July 1). Effects of Porn on Adolescent Boys. Retrieved August 8, 2015, from https://www.psychologytoday.com/blog/sex-lies-trauma/201107/effects-porn-adolescent-boys

10. Snyder, M. (2012, June 1). These Two Traps Are Absolutely Destroying the Next Generation of Young Men in America. Retrieved August 8, 2015, from http://www.infowars.com/these-two-traps-are-absolutely-destroying-the-next-generation-of-young-men-in-america/

11. Neven, T. & Hoose, B. (2006, October 1). Hooked! The Addictive Power of Video Games. Retrieved August 8, 2015, from http://www.focusonthefamily.com/parenting/protecting-your-family/parents-guide-to-video-games/hooked-the-addictive-power-of-video-games

12. Sabina, C., Wolak, J. & Finkelhor, D. (2008). The Nature and Dynamics of Internet Pornography Exposure for Youth. *CyberPsychology & Behavior*, 691-693.

13. Somers, M. (2014, August 1). More Than Half of Christian Men Admit to Watching Pornography. Retrieved August 12, 2015, from http://www.washingtontimes.com/news/2014/aug/24/more-than-half-of-christian-men-admit-to-watching-/?page=all

14. Covenant Eyes. (n.d.). Retrieved August 12, 2015, from http://www.covenant-eyes.com/about-covenant-eyes/corporate-history/mission/

15. Arterburn, S. & Stoeker, F. (2002). Developing Your Battle Plan. In *Every Young Man's Battle: Strategies for Victory in the Real World of Sexual Temptation* (p. 36, 145). Colorado Springs, Colo.: WaterBrook Press.

Game Day 4

1. Ashwill, G. (2010, August 1). Hail Mary. Retrieved July 3, 2015, from http://aga-tetype.typepad.com/agate_type/2010/10/hail-mary.html

2. Burpo, T., & Vincent, L. (2010). *Heaven Is for Real: A Little Boy's Astounding Story of His Trip to Heaven and Back*. Nashville, Tenn.: Thomas Nelson.

3. Hybels, B., & Neff, L. (1998). *Too Busy Not to Pray: Slowing Down to Be with God* (Rev. and expanded. ed.). Downers Grove, Ill.: InterVarsity Press.

4. Omartian, S. (1995). *The Power of a Praying Parent*. Eugene, Or.: Harvest House.

5. Atkins, R. (2006). I've Been Watching You. On *If You're Going Through Hell* [CD]. Nashville, TN. Curb Records.

Game Day 5

1. Metaxas, E. (2013). *Seven Men and the Secret of Their Greatness*. Nashville: Thomas Nelson.

2. Metaxas, E. (2014, December 1). Science Increasingly Makes the Case for God. Retrieved June 20, 2015, from http://www.wsj.com/articles/eric-metaxas-science-increasingly-makes-the-case-for-god-1419544568

3. Cressy Morrison, A. (2004, October 1). Seven Reasons Why a Scientist Believes in God. Retrieved June 21, 2015, from http://www.dlshq.org/messages/sciblgod.htm

Game Day 6

1. About the Air Force: Our Values – airforce.com. (2015). Retrieved June 23, 2015, from http://www.airforce.com/learn-about/our-values/
2. Bowden, M. (1999). *Black Hawk Down: A Story of Modern War*. New York: Atlantic Monthly Press.
3. Joe Landolina: This Gel Can Make You Stop Bleeding ... - TED. (2014, October 1). Retrieved June 23, 2015, from http://www.ted.com/talks/joe_landolina_this_gel_can_make_you_stop_bleeding_instantly
4. Harris, A. & Harris, B. (2015). REBELUTIONIST: In the Pursuit of Purpose.... Retrieved June 24, 2015, from http://rebelutionist.com/
5. Harris, A. & Harris, B. (2008). *Do Hard Things: A Teenage Rebellion Against Low Expectations*. Colorado Springs, CO: Multnomah Books.

Game Day 7

1. McGinnis, A. (1983). *The Friendship Factor*. London: Hodder and Stoughton.
2. Hill, W. (2014, September 1). Why Can't Men Be Friends?. Christianity Today. Retrieved June 29, 2015, from http://www.christianitytoday.com/ct/2014/september/why-cant-men-be-friends-wesley-hill-friendship.html

Game Day 8

1. Tiger Woods says, "I am so sorry" in public apology – CNN.com. (2010, February 1). Retrieved June 30, 2015, from http://www.cnn.com/2010/US/02/19/tiger.woods/index.html

2. Rotondaro, V. (2010, July 1). The Entitled Athlete. Columbia Sports Journalism. Retrieved June 30, 2015, from http://columbiasportsjournalism.com/2010/07/01/the-entitled-athlete/

Game Day 9

1. DeMarco, A. (2012, May 1). Lily Safra's Jewels for Hope Auction Fetches $38 Million, Sets 2 Records. Retrieved September 6, 2015, from http://www.forbes.com/sites/anthonydemarco/2012/05/14/lily-safras

2. AOL. (2014, March 1). Gem Hunter Discovers Rare Rubies Worth $530,000. Retrieved September 6, 2015, from http://www.aol.com/article/2014/03/20/gem-hunter-discovers-rare-rubies-worth-530-000-in-marketplace/20853929/
jewels-for-hope-auction-fetches-38-million-sets-2-records/

3. Ringstaff, M. (2015). 10 Virtues of the Proverbs 31 Woman. Retrieved July 6, 2015, from http://avirtuouswoman.org/10-virtues-of-the-proverbs-31-woman/

4. Caldwell, R. (2012). *33–The Series: A Man and His Design* (Vol. 1). Nashville, TN: Authentic Manhood.

Game Day 10

1. Happell, C. (2013, March 1). A Gumbooted Forrest Gump, Cliff Young Ran His Own Race. Retrieved July 23, 2015, from http://www.theaustralian.com.au/arts/review/a-gumbooted-forrest-gump-cliff-young-ran-his-own-race/story-fn9n8gph-1226603492058

2. Goucher, A. & Catalano, T. (2011, November 1). Modern Day Running Fable (The Cliff Young Story). Retrieved July 23, 2015, from http://www.runtheedge.com/2011/11/modern-day-running-fable-the-cliff-young-story/

3. Dummies.com. The American Football Player's Uniform – For Dummies. (2015). Retrieved July 24, 2015, from http://www.dummies.com/how-to/content/the-american-football-players-uniform.html

4. Higgins, M. (2009, December 1). Football Physics: The Anatomy of a Hit. Popular Mechanics. Retrieved July 25, 2015, from http://www.popularmechanics.com/adventure/sports/a2954/4212171/

5. Fastest ice hockey shot. Guinness World Records. (2009). Retrieved July 25, 2015, from http://www.guinnessworldrecords.com/world-records/fastest-ice-hockey-shot/

6. Hamel, J. (2011, May 1). What is the maximum speed ice hockey players reach? Retrieved July 28, 2015, from https://www.quora.com/What-is-the-maximum-speed-ice-hockey-players-reach

7. Fastest baseball pitch (male). Guinness World Records. (2015). Retrieved July 28, 2015, from http://www.guinnessworldrecords.com/world-records/fastest-baseball-pitch-(male)/

8. Gardner, T. (2010, September 21). How much does it cost to outfit a college football team? Just about $200K. Retrieved July 28, 2015, from http://content.usatoday.com/communities/campusrivalry/post/2010/09/how-much-does-it-cost-to-outfit-a-college-football-team-just-about-200k/1#.VexAREIqDlo

9. Wikipedia. (2015). Scutum (Shield). Retrieved September 15, 2015, from https://en.wikipedia.org/wiki/Scutum_(shield)

Award Ceremony

1. Lewis, R. (2007). *Raising a Modern-Day Knight: A Father's Role in Guiding His Son to Authentic Manhood.* Carol Stream, Ill.: Tyndale House.

2. Nerburn, K. (1999). *Letters to My Son: A Father's Wisdom on Manhood, Life, and Love* (Rev. ed.). Novato, Calif.: New World Library.

Off-Season

1. JJ Weeks Band (2013). Let them see you. On *All Over the World* [CD]. Nashville, TN. InPop Records.

2. Farrar, S. (2003). *Point Man: How a Man Can Lead His Family* (Updated ed.). Sisters, Or.: Multnomah.
3. Farrar, S. (2005). *King Me*. Chicago: Moody.

Artwork

Cover Design by emblem1 on fiverr.com
Icon artwork throughout book designed by Freepik

Acknowledgements

I have learned that it takes a team to complete a book-writing season. I would like to thank the members of my team now:

Head Coach:

God. You gave me the words, ideas, and energy to create this book—from beginning to end. I wrote this book to glorify You, to help good dads become great dads, and to strengthen their father/son relationship. I pray that the words within this book help bring fathers and sons closer to You.

Assistant Coaches:

My bride, Jen: You never once doubted my decision to write this book and encouraged me even on my darkest days. Your prayers were answered. You are a true Proverbs 31 woman, and I loove you so much! DHF and MLIY

My writing coach, Kary Oberbrunner: Had I not met you, this book would not have been written. Thank you for your continued support.

My tribe: the Igniting Souls Tribe: Your insight, experience, suggestions, and support continue to ignite my soul to "show up, filled up." Knowing that I had your support helped me to keep moving forward even on days when I wanted to stop writing.

Offense:

My son, Lincoln: You were always the first one to honestly tell me if the Game Day ideas were worthy or not for this book. You looked forward to the trial runs of each Game Day, being patient with me as I decided whether or not the wording or order of activities was just right. I love you, Link Dawg! Let's play some catch!

My daughter, Hannah: Even though this book did not directly involve you, you supported me 100% of the time, even when I had to sacrifice time with you to write. I love you so much, Nar!

Defense:

My parents, Craig and Sandie LaMaster: You taught me that I could become anything that I wanted and have always supported me.

My sister and brother-in-law, Lisa and Alex Dearborn: You don't know how much it meant to me each time you asked me how my book writing was going. Your thoughtfulness and insight into my early writings has helped me complete this book. I love you both.

Special Teams:

My sister, Holly Hesse: Your talent as a photographer is God-given. Thank you for taking my author's photo and for your support of this book. I love you Holly.

My friends, Nate and Owen Nelson: Nate and Owen, thank you not only for your friendship but also for your support while going through Game Day 7 together. We have to play more disc golf together soon!

Our youth pastor, Pastor Robb Ammerman: You not only supported my writing but have also inspired both of my children to become closer to God. You are an amazing pastor and have a talent for evangelism.

My music station: I would also like to thank K-Love for providing non-stop positive and encouraging Christian music. I wrote my best when I had my ear buds in and was listening to K-Love.

Referee:

My editor, Daphne Parkesian. Your work transformed this book into a polished, finished project. Thank you for your time and expertise.

Fans:

YOU: I would like to thank all of you, the readers, for choosing this book out of the millions of other books on the bookshelf. Without you, the message God chose for this book would not be spread.

DO YOU WANT TO "WEAR" YOUR FRIDAY NIGHT LIGHTS FOR FATHERS AND SONS MEMORIES?

For those of you that have completed your 10-game season, consider purchasing the exclusive FNL4FS memory bands for both you and your son to commemorate your successful season!

If you are interested in purchasing the FNL4FS memory bands, go to:
MarkLaMaster.com

They are reasonably priced and come in small, medium, or large to fit most wrist sizes.

BRING MARK INTO
Your Business Or Organization

Father-Author-Coach-Speaker

Mark's passion is to help good dads become GREAT dads by providing intentional, biblically based activities to help them raise their sons to become godly young men. Mark wants to share his failures and successes to help dads improve their relationship with their sons while at the same time bringing them both closer to God. He will customize each message and training to achieve and succeed the objectives of his clients.

Contact Mark today to begin
the conversation
MARKLAMASTER.COM